More Praise for
The Way of Tenderness

"Zenju Earthlyn Manuel knows both the tyranny of conventional appearances and their ultimate nature. She knows that in order to tread the path to ultimate insight we must use the whole of our ordinary, conventional selves. In this way, our race, gender, and sexuality become sites for our awakening rather than illusions to be transcended. Read her lucid and honest words with attention and with tenderness."
—Jan Willis, author of *Dreaming Me: Black, Baptist, and Buddhist*

"Zenju Earthlyn's book will spark the conversations on race, gender, and sexuality that will move Buddhism in the West to a place of accessibility and inclusivity. For anyone who wants to open their heart to others, this book holds the key."
—Lodro Rinzler, author of *Walk Like a Buddha*

"Zenju Earthlyn Manuel, one of only a small number of African American Buddhist priests, has written a transformative invitation, a breathtakingly courageous and heartfelt call to bring our full humanity—our bodies, our pain, our wounds, our differences—to the path. This is a groundbreaking book, the beginning of a whole new conversation in the Dharma."
—Zenshin Florence Caplow, coauthor of *The Hidden Lamp*

"This is such an unusual book! Yes, it's a Buddhist book, and yes, it's about race, sexuality, and gender as crucial entry-points into the teaching (rather than false identities to be sloughed off). But it's not what you think. Zenju Earthlyn Manuel writes with such gentle poetic intelligence that the reader's experience of the truth she tells feels more like a caress than a jab. Of her own difficult experiences, Earthlyn has forged wise and profound equanimity—a Way of Tenderness."
—Zoketsu Norman Fischer, author of *Training in Compassion*

"Reverend Zenju illuminates many aspects of the First Noble Truth that are invisible to and occluded by the dominant culture of Western Dharma. She does so with force of Truthfulness and the tenderness of Grace. In this way, the offering of her teachings are both the Path and the Fruit."
—Larry Yang, core teacher at the East Bay Meditation Center

"With an authentic and powerful voice, Rev. Manuel offers a unique and fresh perspective on timeless Buddhist truths."
—M. LaVora Perry, author of *Taneesha Never Disparaging*

The Way of Tenderness

AWAKENING THROUGH RACE, SEXUALITY, AND GENDER

Zenju Earthlyn Manuel

Wisdom Publications
199 Elm Street
Somerville, MA 02144 USA
wisdompubs.org

Parts of this book first appeared in *Tell Me Something About Buddhism: Questions and Answers for the Curious Beginner*, Zenju Earthlyn Manuel, Hampton Roads Publishing, 2011.

Library of Congress Cataloging-in-Publication Data
Manuel, Zenju Earthlyn, author.
  The way of tenderness : awakening through race, sexuality, and gender / Zenju Earthlyn Manuel.
     pages cm
  ISBN 1-61429-125-X (pbk. : alk. paper) — ISBN 978-1-61429-149-7 (Ebook)
  1. Buddhism-Social aspects. 2. Race—Religious aspects—Buddhism. 3. Sex—Religious aspects—Buddhism. 4. Sex role—Religious aspects—Buddhism. I. Title.
  BQ4570.S6M45 2015
  294.3'37—dc23

                              2014020585

ISBN 9781614291251   ebook ISBN 9781614291497

21 20 19 18
5 4 3

Author photo by Simbwala Schultz. Cover raku sculpture by Anita Feng. Interior design by Gopa&Ted2, Inc. Set in Sabon LT Pro 10/15.

Wisdom Publications' books are printed on acid-free paper and meet the guidelines for permanence and durability of the Production Guidelines for Book Longevity of the Council on Library Resources.

♻ This book was produced with environmental mindfulness. For more information, please visit wisdompubs.org/wisdom-environment.

Printed in the United States of America.

Please visit fscus.org.

In becoming forcibly and essentially aware
of my mortality, and of what I wished
and wanted for my life, however short it might be,
priorities and omissions became strongly
etched in a merciless light, and what I
most regretted were my silences.
Of what had I *ever* been afraid?
—Audre Lorde

If race, sexuality, and gender are illusions or social
constructs, then what is the tension and ultimate
hatred that arises with regard to them?

Table of Contents

Foreword

BY DR. CHARLES JOHNSON

Ordinary life and Buddhahood have no
     distinction.
Great knowledge is not different from
     ignorance.
Why should one seek outwardly for a treasure,
when the field of the body has its own bright
     jewel?
—Pao-chih, *The Nonduality of Buddhahood*
     and Ordinary Life

Early in this thought-provoking book, Zenju Earthlyn Manuel informs her readers that "The way of
tenderness is not Buddhist, not a religion, not behavior
modification, not a philosophy of life, or a conceptual
view of life. It is not a static path. You will not comprehend this way without laying bare your human conditioning. You will not comprehend it by intellect alone."

Although she is an ordained Zen priest, and author of the splendid book *Tell Me Something About Buddhism: Questions and Answers for the Curious Beginner*, Manuel does not identify her meditation on race, sexuality, and gender as Buddhist. Yet the Dharma (teachings) is present throughout her work. Shakyamuni Buddha was not a "Buddhist." I have read that he simply referred to his disciples as *dhammiko* (followers of dharma). The Dharma is just wisdom. It can be found anywhere and everywhere. No religion or philosophy, Eastern or Western, has a monopoly on wisdom.

As a dhammiko, Manuel is rightly annoyed by the avoidance of this issue in our *sanghas*, our spiritual communities:

> Even though it has been said that we can awaken right where we are, in the very bodies we inhabit, on this planet upon which we walk, we still speak of awakening as if it happens somewhere outside of our particular embodiment in time and space. The silence regarding race, sexuality, and gender in spiritual literature may create the illusion that all is well in our spiritual communities, or that speaking of our unique embodiment in terms of race, sexuality, and gender is not necessary. When the subject is tabled for discussion in spiritual communities, the tension

is palpable, and our inability to approach
it honestly gives rise to frustration, grief,
humiliation, guilt, numbness, blindness, fear,
and rage.

Buddhism teaches the impermanence of all objects
in our ordinary experience. That includes the body.
Unlike most writers on spiritual subjects, Manuel
phenomenologically grounds her meditation there,
for "the dark body in which [she] walks is aging in a
youth-oriented society." That body, our impermanent
and aging flesh, is the third term between consciousness and the world, mediating all of our perceptual
experience. It is the costume that tabernacles consciousness, the temporary clothing that allows others
to sometimes enslave us with their eyes. For this reason Manuel refuses to acquiesce to the polite, often
well-meaning tendency in American sanghas and con-
vert-Buddhist communities to pretend that physical
differences do not matter and are not worthy of discussion. On spiritual paths, we are told, "We are not
our bodies." This is correct from the standpoint of
absolute truth (*paramārtha-satya*). But it is not true
for our daily, lived-experience on the plane of relative
or conventional truth (*samvṛtti-satya*) in a diverse,
multi-racial society where so many suffer from the
three poisons of desire (or greed), ignorance, and
hatred. Therefore, Manuel is compelled to ask, "If the
categories of race, sexuality, gender are illusions or

social constructs then what is the tension and ultimate hatred that arises? How are these things both present and absent? What relationship does race, sexuality, and gender have with spirit? How can we be both tender and liberated? What chases some away from this topic and draws others towards it?"

The questions she presents, much like koans, are unconventional, resembling a trap door that can plunge us into deeper reflections. We all come to Buddhism because we wish to put an end to our suffering, yes. However, all of us come to the Dharma from different places in the world, from different individual and group histories—we come to Buddhism in different bodies. We may be "a child who is bullied at school because of having a flat nose and thick lips," or "a teen who is raped for wearing clothes of the 'wrong' gender." We must answer Manuel's question affirmatively insofar as Samsara is the precondition for experiencing Nirvana. The very suffering caused by racism and discrimination based on embodiment—the predetermined story for dark people—can serve as a powerful catalyst for a person of color taking refuge in the Three Jewels. The worldly fortunes of the flesh can move them to begin questioning, first the falsehoods told about black people (or women or gays) for centuries, then all the lies, assumptions, and presuppositions they have learned and lived in a society that is Eurocentric, materialistic, naively hedonistic, and spiritually broken. We should not pretend to be *blind* to our different forms and conventional identities, but neither should we be *bound* by them. To look courageously at one's historically constituted embodiment and social identity, and to wonder *Why am I treated this way?* or *Who am I?* is a deep-plowing inquiry. It can lead, not to despair, depression, alcohol and drug abuse, or seeing oneself as a victim or pariah, but rather to a transformative kind of mindfulness that reveals to us, as it did to Manuel, how "I have already been given a fully liberated life."

When explaining mindfulness, Bhikkhu Bodhi points out:

> The task of Right Mindfulness is to clear up the cognitive field. Mindfulness brings to light experience in its pure immediacy. It reveals the object as it is before it has been plastered over with conceptual paint, overlaid with inter-pretations. To practice mindfulness is thus a matter not so much of doing but of undoing: not thinking, not judging, not associating, not planning, not imagining, not wishing.

This suspension of judgment, this "letting go" of conceptual paint, informs Manuel's discussion of "tenderness." First, she says, we must recognize that "identity arises spontaneously out of our bodies and minds, and spontaneously evolves in name, meaning, structure and appearance. All of these spontaneously arising things are not fixed and isolated. They arise out of and recede back into the emptiness of our form. Our identities develop as expressions of our not truly knowing what these spontaneous appearances are, and so we name them something or someone. " But such naming need not be divisive or cause suffering, if we understand that everything we think we know is provisional, and if our hearts remain "clear of notions and ideas about others or about anything in life." I have often called this attitude "epistemological humility." In a Buddhist or spiritual sense, it enables Manuel "to allow people to be who they are, without any expectations." Her path of tenderness, then, awakens us to the multiplicity in oneness, to a natural harmony we experience within the body and, most important of all, to seeing that "Our sameness stems from the fact that we share the same life-source as a flower or a bee. But we are nonetheless inherently different in form… The way of tenderness is an experiential, non-intellectual, heartfelt acknowledgement of all embodied difference."

As a good teacher, Zenju Earthlyn Manuel does not expect her conclusions to bring closure to this complex and multi-faceted subject. In fact, she asks that we join her in a continued consideration of race, sexuality, and gender as much needed paths of awakening. After all, "We are more willing to explore and engage our various embodiments when we understand them to be paths to transformation. If we do not anchor our inquiry into life within the undeniable, physical reality in which we live, spiritual awakening will remain far too abstract."

Acknowledgments

Nothing in this world, including our coming into it and leaving it, is done alone. I first honor my ancestors for this life and for their guidance in sustaining heart. I would like to express my gratitude to all of the midwives who cared for this book on its journey into the world: Simbwala Regina Schultz; Arisika Razak; Aishah Shahidah Simmons; Rev. Laura Engelken; Director of Spiritual and Religious Life at Mills College; my teacher Zenkei Blanche Hartman, the former abbess of the San Francisco Zen Center, Kiku Christina Lehnherr; Josh Bartok and the staff—especially Andy Francis, my editor—at Wisdom Publications, who trusted the words and understood so completely the message.

The Way of Tenderness

Not What You Think

—————————— ··❧ ❧·· ——————————

I was hungry when I attended my first Nichiren Buddhist meeting in 1988. I mean that literally. I wanted to go out to eat at a restaurant with two friends of mine, but they insisted that I first attend a Buddhist meeting with them that evening before we ate. With some irritation and a good deal of resistance I sat through the meeting with the group as they chanted *Nam-myoho-renge-kyo*. A month later I was chanting in front of my own Buddhist altar, on which hung a scroll covered with Japanese writing. My Buddhist teachers would ask me "Why do you chant?" I would tell them that I didn't know why. The truth is I was too ashamed to tell them that I chanted because of a deep pain that I could not name.

—————————— ··❧ ❧·· ——————————

A fter about two years of chanting with this pain, I realized that the suffering I felt was part of a

much broader suffering in the world. It was not mine but a suffering that existed before my birth. I recognized that I felt separate from the rest of the world, that I did not belong, and that I was not an acceptable part of the dominant culture because I was so different from the majority in terms of my appearance. The world had structured itself around appearance. The way in which I was perceived and treated depended on a structure of race, sexuality, gender, and class. The perverse power of these structures made my embodiment unacceptable to others and myself. As a result, I was paralyzed by feelings of isolation in my younger days.

I had come not to trust my own innate wisdom. By internalizing the judgments of those who felt that certain types of folks are lesser, I had betrayed myself—I had yielded to oppression. Oppression is a distortion of our true nature. It disconnects us from the earth and from each other. Awakening from the distortion of oppression begins with tenderness: we recognize our own wounded tenderness, which develops into the tenderness of vulnerability and culminates in the tenderness that comes with heartfelt and authentic liberation.

That first experience of tenderness is a cry from deep within our own nature. It compels us to seek out reconnection to the earth and each other. As soon as we are born we begin to drift away from our true nature. We align with established structures that immediately begin to fix our perceptions of others and ourselves. Our lives are shaped by this alignment. Falling into line is a survival mechanism, driven by the suffering that already surrounds us at birth.

As we grow older and more accustomed to the structures that shape us, our own true nature calls to us. This calling can be experienced as a place of separation and suffering. In attending to such suffering, we start down many paths in order to recover the connectedness we lost upon entering the world. For many of us the quest to recover what we feel we have lost extends into social activism, pursuit of spiritual awakening, or both. In my life the quest to recover wholeness and connection has extended into both social activism and spiritual dimensions. In my case, I have experienced spiritual awakening by walking through the fiery gateway of attending to the suffering related to race, sexuality, and gender.

The words "spiritual awakening" conjure images of an experience beyond ordinary life. We may think of spiritual awakening as an experience that transcends this world or that erases all suffering. We may even wish to have an out-of-body or other extreme experience that we might point to as awakening. The wish to spiritually awaken is one of the great natural human desires, ranking right up there alongside the wish to experience love. Yet, most of us don't truly know what spiritual awakening is.

Though we are unclear about what awakening really is, we are likely to feel certain about what it is not. We may feel that it cannot exist within conflict, strife, or pain. We may not feel spiritual awakening is accessible where there is difficulty, suffering, or hardship. Many feel it almost certainly cannot be found amid social struggles related to race, sexuality, and gender. Some may believe that the indignation, ire, and anger that motivate movements of protest only move us "backward" or away from what is more profound about our lives.

But if we were to simply walk past the fires of racism, sexism, and so on because illusions of separation exist within them, we may well be walking past one of the widest gateways to enlightenment. It is a misinterpretation to suppose that attending to the fires of our existence cannot lead us to experience the waters of peace. Profundity in fact resides in what we see in the world. Spiritual awakening arrives from our ordinary lives, our everyday struggles with each other. It may even erupt from the fear and rage that we tiptoe around. The challenges of race, sexuality, and gender are the very things that the spiritual path to awakening requires us to tend to as aspirants to peace.

••⋟ I write this book for an audience spread across many worlds. I tried to keep in mind the academic world, the worlds of social and political activism, the world of spiritual seekers, and people in all worlds who are coming to terms with the color of their skin, their gender, and sexual identities. I hope to arouse in my readers' hearts an urgency to attend to our disconnectedness. I am asking us to look right where we are for timeless wisdom within our struggles of race, sexuality, and gender. I have experienced awakening in many worlds, and across those worlds my awakening came within racist, sexist, and homophobic environments. This is important to note. Awakening does not come in a blind, euphoric, or empty world.

Relatively speaking, I have experienced being "colored," "Negro," "black," "African American," "descendant of Africans," "straight," "bi-sexual," "two-spirited (masculine and feminine)," "tomboy," "lesbian," "dyke," and "poor." I am bi-sexual at heart but have lived in a same-sex or lesbian relationship most of my adult life. I have subscribed to these labels over time, to acknowledge my particular lived experience shaped by its particular suffering. Yes, my bones know the absolute life, unencumbered by labels, fixed perceptions, and appearances. But the absolute life has never been the problem I have to face in the world. In this twenty-first century, many have agreed that race is a construct or illusion used to create racism. It is also acknowledged in some places that sexuality and gender comprise a continua between opposites, and are not fixed states, as was once assumed. The very words "women," "men," "male," and "female" are being transformed to include the many genders between those polarities.

However, simply knowing race to be constructed or an illusion does nothing to change the mind saturated with hatred. To know that there are many ways to live sexually, with or without a prescribed gender, does not affect the extent to which one might be tortured or killed for doing so. Hatred remains potent whether directed at a construct, an illusion, or at the reality of others. Therefore, identity should not be dismissed in our efforts toward spiritual awakening. On the contrary, identity is to be explored on the path of awakening. Identity is not merely of a political nature; it is inclusive of our essential nature when stripped of distortion. In other words, identity is not the problem, but the distortions we bring to it are.

There are many essays, songs, poems, and films that singularly approach race, sexuality, or gender as spiritual subjects. And still there is not enough literature, if any, that addresses embodied race, sexuality, and gender in concert as locations for the experience of spiritual awakening. Even though it has been said that we can awaken right where we are, in the very bodies we inhabit, on this planet upon which we walk, we still speak of awakening as if it happens somewhere outside of our particular embodiment in time and space. The silence regarding race, sexuality, and gender in spiritual literature may create the illusion that all is well in our spiritual communities, or that speaking of our unique embodiment in terms of race, sexuality, and gender is not necessary. When the subject is tabled for discussion in spiritual communities, the tension is palpable, and our inability to approach it honestly gives rise to frustration, grief, humiliation, guilt, numbness, blindness, fear, and rage. We may even gather to commune in our rage, and perhaps to love one another fiercely and tenderly through it.

This tension is our most sacred time. To access this sacred time we must have common ground, we must stand at the water together with all of our problems. Many of us consider being human to be our common ground. This perspective can negate our unique differences and end up causing more tension. Being human is not enough common ground to navigate our challenges. If we could consider our common ground as *trust* we would be more able to remain open to the struggles. What are we trusting? We are trusting that what happens between us is the path by which we must come to awaken as human beings. We must stick to this path with great integrity no matter how difficult.

••⟩ This book is an invitation to explore awakening within the challenges of race, sexuality, and gender. Though issues of race, sexuality, and gender simultaneously are most salient to my experience of hatred (externally and internally), the ideas in this book can be extended to class, physical ability, age, and any other modes of embodiment in relation to which there has been long-held mistreatment and/or systemic oppression. The topic may be overcooked, maybe even burnt, but the scent of it has lingered for hundreds of years. It smells like rage.

The words on these pages came through such rage—
not around it. I am exhausted from the rage. So this
is not a vehicle for me to vent my rage or to present a
new iteration of what many critical theorists and phi-
losophers have already accomplished successfully over
many years. It is not another teaching about getting
along with each other, or about what we ought to do
so we can live happily together. It is not about hope for
some future. It is not about diversity in the tight confines of appearance or best efforts. What I have to say
is not so flat and simplistic. This is not a book about
mindfulness, meditation, or Buddhism, although these
words hover over this book, as they have been refuges
in my life over the decades.

In writing this book I am seeking to step completely
out of the box of what has already been said about
race, sexuality, and gender in both Dharma and social
activist communities. I do not want to stop at Buddha's
teaching on illusion or to continue the political stances
that have been presented for decades. When I engaged
others about this topic, they volunteered their views
of race, sexuality, and gender. I listened for something
new, unfamiliar, uncertain, maybe even something confusing, so that their words would come alive inside me
and shake me loose from my rants and from my time-
consuming pursuit of something to soothe the pain. I
listened for something that might truly transform our
walk in the world together into one without horror and
fear wrapped around the unwanted beings and with-

out false sacredness wrapped around the desired ones. I wanted to hear an unusual, unconventional approach to the topic.

You see, I am a rare member of the second generation descended from relatives who were enslaved in North America. My father and mother were born, respectively, in 1898 and 1910 in rural Louisiana. They told their stories with laughter, but often those happy moments dwindled into stories of lynching, rape, and starvation. They knew hatred up close and protected my two sisters and me the best they could. Yet something lurks in the waters of my gut, just below the surface, and I thought that exploring race, sexuality, and gender within the confines of religious or spiritual community would bring it to the surface. The voices of my ancestors said, "Don't be afraid to say what you need to say."

I am a survivor of the same hatred my parents experienced. The body I inhabit has experienced nearly every category of hatred that exists within this society, directed toward the various unacceptable differences that characterize its appearance. Perhaps it is a result of these experiences that I have paid fierce attention to liberation. And perhaps it is due to the intensity of my suffering, combined with the enchantment that I always felt to be so near, that I want to share the way that has unfurled itself before me, on which I now walk in wellness.

In offering this, I have walked into an old and familiar dialogue. This dialogue rears its head when we feel we are speaking "the truth." In writing this, I walk up to the table of justice with a heart full of spirit. I walk up with a conversation that points directly to the body as spirit and to spirit as body.

I have limited myself throughout this book to numbering only a short string of particular types of embodiment. I do this because in my lived experience the loudest thunder seems to rumble and crack around race, sexuality, and gender, in that order and ranging in frequency from constant to periodic. It is uniquely embodied in these particular forms that I have experienced the struggle to gain access to the resources for living this God-given life. My teachings come from the loud noise of that particular thunder, but I am aware of the simultaneity, interrelationship, and intersection of all forms of embodiment.

The dark body in which I walk is aging in a youth-oriented society. I have struggled with arthritis since the age of eighteen. This disability, which has become more visible as I age, has rendered me fearful and silent when in the company of more able-bodied people. It is difficult to say, "I cannot go with you to the top of the mountain to see those special flowers. Would you bring me a picture?" My body requires material support, so in terms of class I must struggle to maintain a personal economy that defies the larger global capitalist monopoly of the society in which I live and participate. In recognizing the interconnectedness of all embodiment, I find an intimacy within and between all of us that is not sentimental or romantic. From one point of view this intimacy can be expressed as "We are all one." But there is also an interconnected intimacy that is messy, uncomfortable, and difficult, but worthy and liberating to attend to. By the nature of things, we are closer than we would like to be.

Not every question asked in the book will be answered. Unanswered questions leave room for discovery—room in which one can have a direct experience of life. Unanswered questions provoke the journey I want to suggest. In essence, I would like you to join me in exploring race, sexuality, and gender, launching out from our hearts into the liberation promised by many paths. Can we ask about these without expecting answers?

If the categories of race, sexuality, and gender are illusions or social constructs, then what is the tension and ultimate hatred that arises with regard to them? How are these things both present and absent? What relationship do race, sexuality, and gender have with spirit? How can we be both tender and liberated? What chases some away from this topic and draws others toward it?

As someone who enjoys a mystery, I wanted to track the footprints of these invisible monsters that chase us.

Tracking the Footprints
of Invisible Monsters

—————————————— ··❧ ❧·· ——————————————

I was south of Tamil Nadu, India, dreaming. My bed was on fire and I was lying in it. Blue flames shot up around me and I became frightened that I would burn to death. I anticipated the pain and suffering. But I did not burn away. I did not feel any pain or suffering. The flame continued and I just lay there in the blue flames. The body had transformed from its material self into an existence beyond. Going beyond into another existence was not the spiritual awakening. The body coming through the fire and not around it was the awakening for me.

—————————————— ··❧ ❧·· ——————————————

We must come through the fire of our lives to experience awakening. We are all tender no matter where we fall on the continua within race, sexuality, and gender. We are tender in a raw sense, and not necessarily in a soft and gentle way. This tenderness is of a wounded nature. We are all sore from the hatred. Our tenderness is our aching, sensitivity, and ultimately our vulnerability. This raw feeling is not only experienced by those who have been oppressed, abused, and discriminated against. Experiences of hatred, whether giving or receiving it, have no boundaries. The abuser or oppressor also experiences a wounded tenderness. One cannot hate without knowing the experience of it. After all, aren't those who are perceived to be dominant in our society hated too? Can we be tender in the raw sense and still actively walk the path of liberation?

When I was ordained as a Zen priest I was given the dharma name Ekai Zenju, which means Wisdom Ocean (Ekai), Complete Tenderness (Zenju). I could not swim in the ocean, nor did I see myself as tender in the sense of being soft or gentle. I felt the raw and wounded kind of tenderness. For that reason, at first, I embraced the name Ekai because I loved the ocean and visions of it were conjured in the name Ekai. But my teacher told me that the second name is given as the path one is to explore, so I began to call myself Zenju in a quest to discover a lived experience of the name's essence. What is complete tenderness?

It was clear at the beginning of my exploration that I had been hardened by the physical violence leveled against me as a young child and by the poverty with which my parents had to struggle as Louisiana migrants raising three daughters in the wilds of Los Angeles. I had been hurt as a child when I discovered that others saw my dark body as ugly. And as I aged and moved from romantic relationships with men, I lived in fear of being annihilated for taking a woman as a lover and partner in life. I had grown bound to feelings of injustice, rage, and resentment. I held my life tight in my chest, and my body ached with its pain for many years. Depression, unhealthy relationships, dependency on substances to numb the pain, and thoughts of suicide were my responses to the tension. I felt tension between what was imposed upon me and the true nature of life in all of its beauty and perfection. So how does someone who has experienced deep hatred, from within as well as without, become Zenju, Complete Tenderness—a liberated tenderness that is not a wound but complete liberation from the rage that hatred breeds?

I listened to Zen teachers address suffering with Buddha's teachings. I listened for what might help me to face rage and to develop a liberated tenderness. Some suggested that if I "just dropped the labels" I would "be liberated." Some said, "We are delusional; there is no self." Others said, "We are attached to some idea of ourselves." If I could "just let go of being this and that, my life would be freed from pain." I thought for a time that perhaps I was holding on to my identity too tightly. Perhaps, I thought, if I "empty" my mind the pain in my heart will dissolve. What I found is that flat, simplified, and diluted ideas could not shake me from my pain. I needed to bring the validity of my unique, individual, and collective background to the practice of Dharma. "I am not invisible!" I wanted to shout.

Although my teachers taught us the absolute truths of Zen practice, they seemed to negate identity without considering the implications that identity can have for oppressed groups of people. The critique of identity overlooks the emotional, empowering, and positive effects of identity on those who are socially and politically objectified. My own powerful sense of identity, of connection with my ancestors, developed in the Civil Rights and Pan-African movements of the '70s, came through identifying with black people. Leah Kalmanson, a Drake University professor, philosopher, and author, has written, "If this emotional dimension is not brought to the foreground, it threatens to sabotage the practice of identity critique by preventing a person from taking a hard and honest look at herself."[1] Dogen Zenji, founder of the Soto Zen tradition, said, "To study the Buddha way is to study the self." In order to forget the self, we must study it. We must look at the identities that the self is emotionally attached to. This is a life-long practice because identity is ever evolving.

⋯➤ How could I become complete tenderness? Eventually, I accepted that there was no easy answer. I would have to unearth complete tenderness in the midst of the hatred and rage that I felt. So, while participating in a silent seven-day meditation retreat, I began to practice leaving everything—or at least leaving my obsession with things: leaving my aspirations, hopes, dreams, identity, all notions of being this or that, of doing this, that, and the other. I was to say goodbye to these things for seven days. I sat for hours simply breathing in and out. As things came up I would say goodbye, bowing dutifully at the parade of passing thoughts.

During one of the hours of meditation, my deceased mother came to mind. It was as if she had come to silently sit with me. I could not tell her to leave. I immediately began to cry. In that moment I couldn't tell the reason for the tears. It was an upsurge of old pain, harbored from the time of our difficult relationship. How could I be tender given my violent past with her?

I kept breathing and crying, sitting with this vision of my mother. Her face was sweet. She was smiling. She did not appear as the rage-filled, yet beautiful, person that had frightened me when I was young. I opened my eyes to wipe the water pooling between my eyelids. I looked around the room and realized that I had separated from everyone in the room for that moment. I felt they could not possibly be sitting with as much pain as I was. They seemed to be calm and composed. I was not like them. I was a volcano waiting to erupt. I recognized in that moment that old wounds had kept me from fully engaging with folks my entire life. I could be polite or kind to others, but I was unwilling and afraid to experience the wounded tenderness that would have eventually opened into a complete and liberated tenderness. I was unwilling to allow others completely into my heart.

I cried more as the room seemed to darken, and I fused with the darkness. We were all in the dark. In the darkness I was a part of everyone and everything, whether I accepted it or not. Everyone else in the room was as invisible as I was. "I am invisible," I whispered to myself.

In the dark I recognized life without all of the things we impose upon it, and upon each other. As I continued to breathe, I felt a warm breeze near my face, but it was cold and raining outside and there were no open windows or doors. I thought perhaps it was the spirit of my mother. And then I thought, no, perhaps this is how complete tenderness feels when it arrives, having sloughed off rage. When I turned toward the hurt in the silence, I entered a kind of tenderness that was not sore, not wounded, but rather powerfully present. I sat up straight. The silence had tilled hard ground into soft soil. I sunk deep into the soft ground, where the source of life was revealed—wordless, nameless, without form, completely indescribable. And then—I dare to say it—I was "completely tender."

To ease below the surface of my embodiment—my face, my flesh, my skin, my name—I needed to first see it reflected back at me. I had to look at it long enough to see the soft patches, the openings, the soft, tender ground. Would I survive the namelessness—without my body, without my heart—while engaging the beautiful, floral exterior of my life? Fear and caution were attempting to shut down the experience of uncoupling my heart from mistreatment and discrimination—from the disregard, hurt, and separation that I experienced and accepted as my one-sided life. I was going back to the moment before I was born, when I was connected to something other than my parents or my people. The uncoupling from hatred within and without squeezed my chest, restricting blood flow in my neck. It felt as though I were having a heart attack. Even namelessness requires breathing. I could not remain in that vastness without inhaling and exhaling. So I breathed hard and deep for some time, and I was eventually escorted to the emergency room to see if, in fact, I was having a heart attack.

Complete tenderness almost wiped me out. And perhaps it does wipe "you" out—that "you" that suffers so, that "you" unaligned with the Earth body. Still, what does liberation mean when I have incarnated in a particular body, with a particular shape, color, and sex, which can be superficially viewed as an undesirable, unacceptable, or ugly image of human life? Enlightenment, as it has for sages and prophets down through the ages, emerges through bodies. Our bodies make us visible, even though many strive toward a spiritual transcendence in which we imagine we will become invisible. For me, that brief experience of invisibility attained deep in meditation was but a moment of awakening to the beauty of life, and it existed right within my extremely visible self. When recognition and awareness always occur within bodies, how can we ignore race, sexuality, and gender?

•❧ The pain of disregard was embedded early in my life, growing roots that eventually proved to be invasive and dangerous to the core of my being. So for most of my life I have participated in the political, sociological, and psychological analyses used in hopes of mending the wounds. My mind grew so crowded with "isms" that my ability to intellectually constrain them all was impossible. I ended up at war with myself because I fell into almost every marginal group one can imagine. It seemed to be a cold war in workshops where many experts, whether they meant to or not, seemed demanding and often harmful in the ways they dealt with racism, homophobia, classism, ableism, ageism, or any situation that would oppress one group of living beings based on erroneous ideas of superior and inferior people.

Although we learn through discomfort, I experienced the demanding nature of the work of mending wounds as imposing correctness, as controlling my own and others' thoughts. There was no "correctness" that could sustain "correctness" over decades. As we evolved in our thinking, our theories and philosophies changed. Yet we had not considered transformation from the very base of our rage, from the ground of our perceptions of each other. No matter how much they aimed to bring an end to the suffering of oppression, none of these political or social paths seemed capable of transforming suffering at its core. So I deepened my path to include the mystery of life, which led me to the gateway of Dharma.

Growing up, I had never been asked who I was. I was told who I was. There was no room for self-discovery. I was told from a young age that my life was going to be a particular way because of my dark skin. And in fact I did experience the struggles of growing up as a black girl child. Based on what I experienced, I accepted the story of what was predetermined for black people, feeling completely destined for tragedy. I imagined that I would have to fight all my life to get what I wanted out of it. I imagined dying unfulfilled. I believed that I did not have access to the resources for life, and that access to them was being denied or withdrawn by the powers that be. All of that was true from one narrow perspective. But there was more.

No one informed me that who I was had nothing to do with the way I appeared to others. In fact I believed that who I was had everything to do with how I appeared to others. So I spent a great amount of time and money on appearance, education, and "appropriate" political and spiritual engagement. Only in the deep silence of meditation did I begin to disbelieve that I was born only to suffer. Eventually after many years of sitting meditation, I recognized the root of my self-hatred, both external and internal, as a personal and collective denial or denigration of the body I inhabited. I clearly could see a distorted identity unaligned with the earth I was becoming more and more disconnected from my own heart. In the silence of meditation I could see that, in being an object of hatred, I lived my life as an object of everything and everyone. A thing can be dressed up and stripped down depending on situations and circumstance. Denial and acceptance was based on being a good or bad object in the view of others. This was not life.

··❧ I read in a book of Buddha's teachings called the *Dhammapada* that:

> Mind precedes all mental states.
> Mind is their chief; they are all mind-wrought.[2]

Although Buddha was addressing his monks with these lines, we can easily read his words in reference to the collective mind of our society as it views race, sexuality, and gender. When individuals in our society speak or act out of hatred against a whole group of people based solely on superficial appearance, it is a reflection of the mental state of our whole society. We don't escape because we are not the ones hating. When whole groups of people are subject to genocide, massacre, slavery, or other atrocities based on perceived unacceptable differences, we see a society cracking and crumbling. We can recognize this in our personal lives. We ourselves fall into hatred when, because of someone's appearance, we seek to render them or the group to which we feel they belong, invisible. It is also an act of hatred to grant privilege, superiority, and favor to a person or group of people because of their embodiment.

We see hatred working in the heart of our society when a sixteen-year-old black male is shot to death—with eleven rounds fired by six white officers—because the police say he was adjusting the waistband of his pants in a "suspicious way." We see hatred working in the heart of our society when a gang of black males murder a black transgender rapper and dump the body in a landfill. We see hatred working in the heart of our society when women are gang raped simply because they are women. We see hatred working in the heart of our society when the homeless are stabbed on the street because they are ugly, destitute, and unpleasant to look at. Fear of particular bodies breeds hatred, and hatred breeds monstrous acts. This is the mind of a society that breeds hatred.

How could a path to spiritual liberation possibly unfold if we turn away from the realities that particular embodiments bring? To confront hatred with spirituality is to confront the way we view race, sexuality, gender, or whatever form of embodiment we are as living beings. To provide a meaningful path to spiritual liberation, spirituality must acknowledge the body and the denigration of certain types of bodies in the world.

We cannot close our eyes to these phenomena if we really want to be awake and aware.

For many, spiritual paths should tend toward the invisible, the unseen. With this view it is easy to mistake a favorable blindness—not seeing skin color, gender, etc.—for seeing an invisible truth of life. We may even consider this blindness to be a higher state of being. But the wisdom in my bones says that we need this particular body, with its unique color, shape, and sex, for liberation to unfold. There is no experience of emptiness without interrelationship. In meditation the wisdom deep in my bones tells me that I do not have to fight against someone or something to gain my life. I have already been given a fully liberated life. In stillness I glimpse the freedom that is already there. With each glimpse I touch the earth, I grow more deeply rooted in the source from which the wisdom of spiritual teachings has always emerged.

Of course, many ancient spiritual teachings do not specifically address race, sexuality, and gender in the ways that we do today. Still, differences between ancient tribes, castes, and ethnic groups have been sources of conflict forever. Happiness and pain, loss and gain, want and plenty have been bound up with superficial distinctions between people based on their embodiment all throughout history. In other words, the basic awareness of the human condition and the inspiration to resolve persistent pains that have been shared by spiritual teachers down through the ages comes through seeing the challenge that appearance presents to living beings, and how it shapes their lived worlds.

Today, using such ancient teachings to promote favorable blindness, we end up turning away from the very types of lived experiences that motivated such teachings to begin with. We must look our embodiment in the face in order to attend to the challenge it presents. Only then will we come to engage each other with *all* of what we are—both the relative and the absolute, the physical and the formless.

••❥ The way of tenderness spontaneously presented itself in my ordination name, Zenju—Complete Tenderness. The name was a revelation. It revealed to me that I needed to move from hatred into directly experiencing life as it is, without distortion or manipulation. It revealed to me that I too, in all of my darkness, could experience life as the breath that it is. The way of tenderness is not Buddhist, not a religion, not behavior modification, not a philosophy of life, or a conceptual view of life. It is not a static path. You will not comprehend this way without laying bare your human conditioning. You will not comprehend it by intellect alone. You will not arrive at the door of complete tenderness through manipulative words or through passivity. You cannot be trained or taught, at any cost, to walk this path. It cannot be practiced. I repeat: It cannot be practiced. There are no diplomas or progress reports on whether you have succeeded in not being racist or sexist. Complete tenderness simply rises up as an experience void of hatred—for oneself or otherwise. As a matter of fact, I can barely write about it. Still, I feel compelled to speak of what is in my bones for the sake of bringing back the connectedness we were all born with.

The way of tenderness appears on its own. It comes when the events of your life have rendered you silent, have sat you in the corner, and there is nothing left to do but sit until the mental distress or confusion about who you are or who you are not passes. The way of tenderness may present itself when rage is so palpable that you are dizzy with it. It may come as a lion's roar. The way of tenderness comes even when failing to fight for our lives is what we fear the most. Complete tenderness arrives even if we have no desire to sink beneath the appearance of things, including our own identities and aspirations.

The way of tenderness is an experiential, non-intellectual, heartfelt acknowledgment of all embodied difference. It is a flexibility of perception, rather than a settling into belief. It brings affirmation of life, rather than of suffering, center stage. It keeps alive the vow not to kill in a way that has nothing to do with being vegetarian or not. It is social action. It is a way to overcome what feels much stronger than us, and what seems to pull us apart so that we are not well. It is an acknowledgment of the unfolding experience of life that is effortlessly ever-present in all living beings, and yet it does not deny the uniqueness or similarities of our embodiment. It simply arises along the path of life, if we allow it.

The tenderness that arose in my life brought with it a liberated and well-hearted engagement with life; it was a transformation of pent-up anger, rage, and disappointment. Instead of sinking into pain and separation I did a very scary thing. I allowed tenderness—a gentle opening, a softness of mind and body—to surface. I followed that opening until the way of tenderness unearthed itself as a liberated path. It is a natural, organic, innate medicine, or teaching *within the body* itself. I used to be afraid of being seen in this softness, afraid of being viewed as "soft." How could I be tender in the liberated sense, and be strong and safe? How could I meet disrespect or disregard with tenderness? How could I trust it? How can I be tender when there is war?

How can I *not* be tender when there is war? When I contemplated being tender in this way, I realized that it did not equal quiescence. It did not mean that fiery emotions would disappear. It did not render it acceptable that anyone could hurt or abuse life. Tenderness does not erase the inequities we face in our relative and tangible world. I am not encouraging a spiritual bypass of the palpable feelings that we experience. The way of tenderness is an intangible elixir for the clogged arteries in the heart of our world. I say that complete tenderness is an experience of life that trusts the fluidity of our life energy and its extension into those around us. On the way of tenderness we allow rage and anger to flow in and out again, in and out again, instead of holding on to it as proof of being human. We can let go of stockpiling our rage for fear that our suffering might go unrecognized or that we'll appear apathetic or naïve. I say that a liberated tenderness is a way of lessening and finally removing the potency of our tragic pasts as sentient beings. I say that this way is what will change what it is within us that leads us to annihilate the unacceptable differences between us.

··❧ **I remember when I was a child my father tipped his hat to strangers on the path.** I would smile and nod along with him, and the strangers would nod back. What I received in the nod back from the strangers was recognition that we were living beings. It meant that my undeniable difference was nonetheless seen as part of the landscape of life. To be recognized as a living being without so much as a spoken word was to acknowledge a life that cannot be seen in a mirror but rather is seen only in each other.

This kind of acknowledgment, the passing nod along the way, is an old southern tradition. My Louisianan parents taught me that in nodding "hello" you let folks know that you see them—not their faces, but their lives. Everyone performed this acknowledgement, despite the other's embodiment. We did it right in the midst of an environment in which harmful discrimination was everywhere. That act came from a place that ignored for a moment the perceived ugliness of the human species. We didn't stop to think whether or not we would acknowledge a particular person. We just did it, regardless of whom it was for. Of course, if we were to stop and think about the person, a whole range of emotions might surface. But if we took the tender gesture of the nod as given, without preconceptions, the nod was just a nod. We honored each life. In the *zendo* (Zen meditation hall) we bow with our hands joined. This is an acknowledgment of something beyond "you and I."

If I were to define the way of tenderness, I would say that it is acknowledgment—acknowledging and honoring all life and all that is in the world, fully, with heart and body. This acknowledgment is wordless and is expressed in a deeply felt nod to everything and everyone—an inner bow to life, so to speak. The way of tenderness is a response from below the surface of what appears to us when we are seeing, hearing, touching, smelling, tasting, or thinking. It is a response beyond the mind, but of the body. It rises up quite naturally, without preconception, without our knowing the reason for the tears, fierce anger, or laughter that come with it. With the welling up of tenderness, we are like newborn babies simply experiencing the sensations of being alive. It is our own unique experience.

⋯❧ **The way of tenderness is not a method for how to behave, how to be kind, or how to transform our behavior with each other.** By this point, we have grown past formulas, techniques, and strategies that teach us how to honor life. It is time to recognize that we already know something of ourselves. The question is: Can we integrate the heavens that our hands reach up toward and the earth our feet are planted in? There is far too much hate in the world and far too many lives are snuffed out because of it. When we fully know in our hearts who we are as living beings, not only emotionally, psychological, politically, or socially, we can share a deeply felt, visceral acknowledgment of each other. We can submit our interrelationship to the blue flames, unafraid of being burned away.

We have bodies so that we can engage life. We need our bodies to experience our hearts and minds. Most of us will not transcend them until death. If the body can withstand the arising and ceasing of pain and suffering, there is no need to transcend it. We need to transcend, instead, our belief that spirituality does not include the body. Of course the body would hold no interest for us were we not interested in awakening, which happens through this body. Because we long for and enjoy experiences of awakening, the body is deeply interesting to us. Given the deep relationship between awakening and the body, why not explore the surfaces of this body—its race, sexuality, and gender—in relation to awakening at its heart?

I do not explore race, sexuality, and gender separately, because others have already done that quite well and because I intend not to focus on critical theory or analyses but instead on the personal experience of the heart-mind, body, and spirit. So rather than separately addressing race, sexuality, and gender, I explore them as integral in the sense of their simultaneity. The way of tenderness is to see such interrelationship among us. Here I will explore awakening to the challenge of embodiment through two states of being in interrelationship: (1) multiplicity in oneness and (2) the body as nature. These two states of being are only meant to assist dialogue, not to set in stone a path that is inherently experiential and variable according to each life. Briefly, "multiplicity in oneness" indicates an awareness that oneness includes difference, and "the body as nature" indicates an awareness that the body itself is an inherited form of nature. These two also indicate that identity exists, and that there is a natural identity that exists alongside contingent sociopolitical and emotional ones.

Multiplicity in Oneness

·◦✧ ✧◦·

One of the things I loved most as a child was to swing in our backyard for hours. I pushed back and forth until the height of the swing almost reached the top of the tallest palm tree. This was how I spent my time contemplating life. The more I thought about the things that happened at school, home, or church, the higher the swing climbed into the air. Swinging helped to move the pain that had no words. I rocked back and forth through the confusion between love and hate. The wind passed over me, a small, innocent, black girl-child in a society that created myths about differences.

Unworthiness, invisibility, loss of intimacy, isolation, neglected intuition, lack of love, intense fear, overwhelming distrust, and a loss of voice—all life-threatening symptoms of the disease of systemic oppression. When my heart was full, I held my breath and jumped out of the swing at its highest arc. I loved flying through the air and the feeling of the wind rushing up underneath my dress. I was familiar

with the landing strip because I had flown often. Most times
I landed right on my feet.

Wide-eyed and curious I questioned the horrors
of life. I thought deeply about the pain in the
world. In 1988, when I first entered the Dharma path
laid out in the Buddha's teachings, I didn't trust that
the teachings could ever touch the pain in my heart. Yet
I, with my Christian upbringing, walked through the
door of the Buddhist temple. I immediately grieved the
missing sense of community found in African-Ameri-
can influenced Christianity of the '60s and '70s, based
on a shared history of dehumanization—specifically
slavery. The black churches of my youth built a Christianity founded on an African spirituality that was not
an individual experience but a communal quest to discover a kind of wholeness that is realized only in community. The black church was the collective soul of the
people—an animating and integrative power that constituted both the individual and collective experience. It
was a spirituality dedicated to equality and preservation
of community, embedded within a collective historical
existence.

To me, being Christian by sensibility was being
black. So entering the path of Buddha felt like leaving
the African American community. However, my physical departure was at least made easier by the funda-

mentalist approach to Christ's teachings taken at my church, its inability to embrace women as ministers, and their fear of sexual differences clearly embodied in some of its members. Yet I continued to yearn for that collective, communal experience on the spiritual path.

I had no real desire to be Buddhist, to chant, or to meditate. I was clueless when Buddhism presented itself through friends in the Japanese Nichiren tradition. The teachings softened my heart, and the promise of inner peace kept me in front of the *Gohonzon* scroll given out by Soka Gakkai. After fifteen years with Soka Gakkai, in the blink of an eye, I found myself sitting in silence in a zendo. When I heard Dharma teachers of African descent speaking at an auspicious retreat for African Americans at Spirit Rock Meditation Center, it felt natural to move from Soka Gakkai to Soto Zen. When I entered the temple, a Zen chant expressing the determination to save all beings inspired me to deepen my quest to end suffering, especially the suffering of dehumanization. The words liberation, compassion, love, and wisdom fell like drops of medicine on my heart.

However, it wasn't long before I discovered within the Zen Buddhist community the unspoken expectation that a spiritual person transcends notions of race, sexuality, and gender, and all other forms of embodiment. To speak of identity was a mark of being unenlightened. I was left on my own to make sense of ancient teachings in my life in this modern world. In the modern world we are left to contend with hatred based on embodied differences and the histories that come with them. Am I to let go of the shared historical past of slavery but continue to hold on to the uplifting shared histories or cherished lineages of the ancient spiritual communities of another? There is multiplicity in the spirit of oneness. This I knew in my bones.

••❥ Childhood experiences of a communal way of life taught me to acknowledge multiplicity in oneness as a way of tenderness—a way of walking free and well. Despite preferences, despite opinions for or against what might be held close to the heart, our way of life included everyone and everything. I was raised on the teaching that God was love. But the communal consciousness of multiplicity in oneness in many black churches seemed to disappear with the rise of the feminist and the gay rights movements. The civil rights movement was viewed as superior to these. I discovered then that I would never preach in my church because they did not allow women ministers, and that I would become a pariah if I were to come out as a woman who loved women. This atmosphere deeply challenged what I knew in my bones about God's love.

The truth is that the liberation of Christ is inclusive of women as ministers and LGBQTI followers of Christ's path. Since those early days of the feminist and gay rights movements many black churches have broadened their embrace of these issues. Still, many black churches remain rooted in an extreme funda-mentalist position, and many LGBQTI people remain rooted in opposition to them. These extremes are gen-erally not spoken of in Buddhist communities, but this does not mean that the same polarities don't exist there too. The practice of observing silence, central in many meditation communities, can have an adverse effect on useful discourse. We don't speak openly of oppositions that stand as boldly in the room as the many statues of Buddha. The idea of unity may lead us to think that differences, as superficial distinctions, are counter to the teachings of universality or interrelationship. There is multiplicity within our relationship with each other.

Multiplicity in oneness does not mean that prefer-ences, opinions, likes, dislikes, or even hate cease to be present. Everything is here. Challenges arise when we cling to one extreme among multiplicities, unwill-ing to acknowledge the presence of difference. It isn't always necessary to engage that difference, but giving it an "inner bow" allows us to experience the whole land-scape of oneness. By not acknowledging difference, we unwittingly exaggerate the difference until it screams to be acknowledged.

··❧ **Inclusiveness underlies oneness.** Being aware of the multiplicity in oneness requires that we recognize the collective nature of our lives. It is crucial that we see the variety of lived experiences within oneness in order to see who we really are as living beings. We have mistaken our sameness for being human. Our sameness stems from the fact that we share the same life-source as a flower or a bee. But we are nonetheless inherently different in form. When we speak of race, sexuality, and gender—when we speak of our embodiment—*we speak of all of us*, not just "those people" over there.

Some misperceive "difference" to refer only to people of color, "race" to refer only to black men, "sexuality" to queer people, "gender" to white women, "class" to those with have inherited wealth or those who live in poverty, and so on. And notice black women are hardly considered on the continuum at all. Whether or not we see ourselves in terms of these groups, we all participate in these consciously and unconsciously created constructs (or delusions, if you see them in that way). Because there are multiple expressions of life, we all partake in race, sexuality, and gender. We all partake in the nature of oneness and the challenges that exist within it. We are all raced, sexualized, classed, and so on. This can be difficult to see.

The body, distinct in its appearance and character, is the location of awakened experience. Inclusivity lies at the heart of understanding multiplicity in oneness as a way of tenderness, as a way of facing the challenges of the body as the location of awakened experience. We may think that oneness should exclude marks of diversity like race, sexuality, and gender, yet oneness is inclusive of everything in our lives. We are interrelated despite our varied embodiments and ways of living.

Race, sexuality, and gender are not merely labels or categories, but involve tangible lived experiences for each of us. We cannot experience life without a body, and we live our lives with the categorical names given to our bodies.

You may not share this line of thought, and feel that the topic of this discourse is only for those who suffer within particular groups, and therefore have an ax to grind. We may attempt to refrain from identity out of fear of opposition and conflict, not seeing its transformative capacity. We all react, respond, yell out, hold back, cry, laugh, or curse, when these so-called labels are activated. If race, gender, and sexuality are merely labels, merely words, we should be capable of moving through life without being affected by them, as if they all were truly only illusions. Some say that these are only words, and pretend to be unaffected and uninterested until the words include or exclude them, until they find that they, too, are affected and experience a sense of harmful discrimination.

We must acknowledge the relevancy of our lived experience, even within the absoluteness of our being, beyond our material embodiment. There is a relational self on the path of spirit. In other words, our identities in terms of race, sexuality, and gender cannot be ignored for the sake of some kind of imagined invisibility or to attain spiritual transcendence. We are not capable of being "unembodied" Selves, nor are we meant to be. We cannot become the Self that we cannot touch, that does not suffer, that has no name, no color, no eyes, no ears, no nose, no tongue. No matter how many labels we drop we cannot become that Self.

••❧ I once saw a news panel on how to be an ally to those who are systematically oppressed in society. The panel was comprised of a diverse group of selected activists recognized for their work in the area of social justice. When asked how one becomes an ally to the marginalized, with a big smile, one man said, "I won the lottery because I'm white, male, and heterosexual. So I must use my privilege to help others." This man had learned to acknowledge that privilege exists for some in our society, but I was stunned by his claim that his particular embodiment was actually richer than those of others. I was further stunned by the lack of response to his claim by the moderator and the brown and black activists, who seemed to implicitly agree that his embodiment was "better," and that he bore the great responsibility that comes along with the great power afforded by his body. While I did understand that the panel was agreeing with his front row seat in political power structures of our country, it was the joy on his face in regards to his embodiment and owner-ship of privilege that said he somehow embraced white superiority.

This young man's claim is a useful example that allows us to see how labels create a lived experience, and how that lived experience affects others. The absence of a collective or communal view of his life contributed to the shaping of the lives of those who didn't "win the lottery" because of the color, sex, etc. He spoke as if he were lucky by birth (it takes luck to win the lottery, after all), and that his luck set him apart from those who have no luck—those who have to advocate in order to be treated as human. I don't mean to downplay the gift that this young man was giving. I am simply pointing out how even in his giving and the black and brown activists receiving, we perpetuate notions of light as superiority and dark as inferiority, and how this leads directly to a mentality of hatred. Such mentalities lead us further away from the possibility that being born black or brown is also winning the lottery.

If he won the lottery in his birth, then we all have, because we have all been born. It is not the responsibility of one kind of people to liberate another while holding on to the winnings. By seeing some groups only as "allies" we cause them to appear to be "carriers of peace and wellness," and those who fight for what ought to be their birthright to be "carriers of pain, suffering, and disruption." There is no single group of people who are "carriers of the oneness of nature." No one group or person embodies nature or possesses it in a way that allows it to be defended or handed over. We have all won life and the right to live it is our birthright. This is the true essence of social justice—the spirituality of it.

⋅⋅❥ **While all of us may not identify with labels of race, sexuality, gender, class, age, disability, and so on, we all cling to such appearances because of our embodied interrelationship.** An acknowledgment that these constructions were created together and are cultivated together is crucial for this old dialogue to open and breathe, and to be life affirming and transformative in its opposing nature. It's about whether or not we are interested in such aspects of life, about whether we will attend or neglect the collective suffering of all living beings.

If we have created "race," we are all involved in the lived experience of it, whether we individually view ourselves in terms of race or not. When we are treated by others or act ourselves with a consciousness of race, we can count on an impact of that consciousness on everyone we interact with. If oppression is a particular kind of suffering for some, then it is a general type of suffering for all. Do we all acknowledge this suffering? No. Are we all tender, in the sense of wounded soreness, to it? Because of the nature of our interrelatedness, the answer is yes. Whether we are aware of it or not, we are all connected to this wounded tenderness in some way. So why can't we use it in the service of liberating action? We usually suppress our tenderness, because it leaves us far too exposed. But the feeling of woundedness is not the complete experience of tenderness. The complete experience of tenderness is to acknowledge that within the seamless life shared between us, we cannot parcel out hate to some without affecting the whole of humanity. When we reach that kind of tenderness—complete tenderness—liberation is won.

Race, sexuality, and gender are born out of an awareness that "I am this." The feelings and perceptions that follow this awareness give rise to an experience of life as appearance-based. Race, sexuality, and gender are perpetuated when past experiences of them carries forward into the present. We carry historical atrocities, such as slavery, genocide, massacres, or holocausts, in our collective memory. The memory of these tragedies persists in society, creating unexamined biological myths. Biological myths (a term I borrow from Michelle M. Wright, author and professor at Northwestern University) are stories created about certain groups of people that lack accurate historical perspective or content. Bigotry and supremacy of all kinds emerge from biological myths. More importantly, an invisible hatred is justified by these myths, and the myth obscures our ability to directly experience one another and to see the oppression that functions as the norm in society.

The biological myths associated with my particular embodiment run rampant in our society. I have been mistaken for "the help," a thief, a thug, a mammy (or someone to milk when in pain), an uncontrolled sexual object, and for a child (even though I am the age of most grandmothers). From my side, I have walked as an author, have been a nonprofit executive for twenty-five years, and am now an ordained Zen priest. I don't name these earthly accomplishments to elevate myself. I name them to show that we cannot truly see each other. Even these things are not who I really am. We see the roles that we play and the biological myths that come with them. The roles I play in life are not life itself. The nature of my life expresses itself in many ways.

Biological myths obstruct our capacity to see multiplicity in oneness. Perhaps by relieving ourselves of ungrounded stories we can unload political concerns that have swollen nearly to bursting. Perhaps we can roll the dynamic of accepted and unaccepted differences among us from our heads into our bodies, into our hearts, to better feel, speak to, and encounter each other—even as we may only truly meet ourselves for the first time—in stillness, in ritual, or in ceremony. Not blind to color, deaf to anger and rage, ashamed of history, but ever present to the ways in which we have rendered some lives dispensable and others not. How can we use our spiritual paths to lead ourselves out of ignorance and deception? Is purification through meditation enough? I say we need more as many of us struggle to sustain a commitment to purification, whether it is meditation, praying in sweatlodges, indigenous ritual, or ceremony. We need the connectedness we once knew.

When we recognize that we are all a part of the collective injury of hatred, we begin to face our unexamined fears. We do not have to go far to find ourselves in the midst of human struggles based on unacceptable differences. This struggle is an intimate tension inherent to life, and yet for some reason it is often considered tangential to contemporary spiritual teachings. Within many Buddhist communities, discussions of difference gravitate toward a superficial sameness or "no self," without realistically addressing the suffering that has happened—that is happening—among human beings. Such suffering, when explored in Buddhist communities, is treated as a personal issue rather than as a collective injury. Those who shed light on particular mistreatments become the focus, rather than the mistreatment itself. It is quite possible for the majority of a community to stand aloof and watch, as if they are not affected by the mistreatment. This kind of experience can become the source of longstanding divisiveness and isolation.

••❧ There is nothing more powerful than looking out on nature and seeing the varied expressions of life, taking in its myriad forms that touch our hearts or that disturb them. We ourselves are just as magnificent as anything expressed in nature as nature. We need only be that magnificence. Yet when we try to "be" magnificent, discrimination and discernment enter into our minds. We leave out who and what we think is not magnificent. We exclude whatever we judge to be lesser in our minds, which leads to manipulative action and to formation of ideologies that blind us to the true beauty of ourselves as nature. The organic evolution of seeing ourselves as part of nature, as beautiful as nature, is what we have been working toward as human beings from the beginning of our time on this planet.

Yet we constantly move against each other, which is to move against nature. The inability to see the true beauty of nature in ourselves, as ourselves, causes injury, assault, and war for all sentient creatures. From our beginnings we have been confronted by our differences, and our inability to see them as the natural order of things has allowed discomfort and fear to develop in our societies and has turned us against ourselves. The destruction wrought by this process reaches beyond our own species to affect other living beings as well. We have been concerned with our personal and particular needs without much care for what it costs others. Who will pull the plow, harvest the crop, build, and sacrifice their land, culture, and bodies for us?

Fortunately our intelligence allows us to clearly see this destruction and disconnection. And we have, down through the ages, developed many means to attempt to heal, mend, and atone for our actions. Yet while our spiritual paths have assisted us, our aspirations to be "better" human beings may inadvertently hinder us. To be "good" people we tend to bypass the messiness of our lives in order to enter the gate of tranquility. Can the gate of tranquility really be as we imagine it? No matter which way we approach peace, it seems we must cross the burning threshold of human conditioning to enter it. So, before we leap to the universal, the true essence, or spirit, why not start where we are as human beings? We must carve a path through the flames of our human condition. We must see it for what it is, and bow to it—not a pitiful bow, but a bow of acknowledgment. By acknowledging our human condition, we acknowledge that we might not know how to end hatred and that we are not superheroes; we are human beings.

··➣ **Once at a retreat a white woman commented that the only black people "like me" that she had seen were on television.** At the time I hadn't seen any people like myself on television, so I didn't know what people she could have been referring to, and of course I didn't ask. She could have meant it as a compliment, but I interpreted it negatively and was annoyed. I simply let the comment drop, like a dead leaf falling to the ground, without responding to it. I knew in my head that we were encountering persistent images of each other based on a collective societal history that goes unspoken in spiritual communities.

We experienced each other through our material bodies and perceptions of them as a black woman and a white woman. We did this in an environment that had taught us that race, sexuality, and gender are illusions, and yet I felt them; the body said that they were real. And yet we were both included in the single field of nature. Both aspects of our perception were true—the illusory and nonillusory. The path of spirit is grounded in the embodied experience. Even in separation there is inclusion: she was included in the blackness I felt, whether she knew it or not, when she commented on the blackness that appeared before her, and I was included in her whiteness. The oneness did not disappear despite our awareness of difference. It was there, waiting to be recognized, whether we experienced oneness or not.

There is room within awareness to establish human relationships, if we are willing. Our engagement with others would be more direct if it were done with an honest internal acknowledgment of the fears and frustrations we bring to them. We often pretend we are not afraid or that we are not angry. Can we engage honestly with our fears and frustrations? Not that we have to share our inner world cross-culturally, but let's say the woman and I were friends, what would have happened if she said, "I am afraid of you because I have never engaged anyone like you before," and I said, "It angers me when folks are afraid of me and they don't even know me"? I would have liked her to first take the time to develop a friendship or context in which race could be encountered rather than blurting out words in regards to my being black.

If we are to truly encounter each other with integrity we must engage with a true intimacy that allows for the expression of guilt, anger, or fear—not to each other, necessarily, but to ourselves. If we are willing to expose our full range of emotions, we must first establish true friendships or relationships as foundations upon which honest dialogue about race, sexuality, and gender can be built. And we must establish those relationships without the agenda of wanting to investigate another's blackness, queerness, etc. The friendship must be integral and genuine. It is within friendship or relationship that a liberated and complete tenderness is experienced.

We often want to cross cultural boundaries or to become allies without taking the needed steps toward real intimacy, without considering the challenges of race, sexuality, and gender in developing authentic human relationships. How can someone ally with me without knowing anything about what it means to befriend a black lesbian woman in this society? How could someone speak for anyone else without ever having deeply encountered that person?

••❧ **Here's another experience I've had of being awake to the multiplicity in oneness.** My beloved and I were at a popular grocery store. We were ready to order breakfast and were the only customers at the counter. It was clear that we were together as a couple. We stood there for quite a long time waiting to be served. The server, brown skinned but not black like us, stood behind the counter gazing off. She looked at us for a moment and then gazed off again, as if we weren't there.

She simply stares out waiting for customers, but not the ones standing in front of her. We move into her field of vision to make eye contact with her. She just stands there. She looks past us. Soon, a young man comes, brown like her, not black like us. He steps to the counter without asking if we've been helped. The server quickly takes his order. It's 2012, not 1959! The familiar and visceral feeling of being mistreated spreads in my chest and head. Fire rises to my crown and brings down grief in its aftermath—the ancient grief of a young girl who used to jump high into the air from her swing and land on her feet, hoping her pain would be dissolved in flight.

Unlike the white woman at the retreat, the server acted without saying a word about our blackness, our queerness, or anything at all about our embodiment. We perceived her disregard directly through our own experience, palpable in our awareness of our own bodies. Some would say that the fire about my head meant that I had taken the situation personally. Some may say I was conjuring up the discrimination. Yet there was a wider psychic field beyond all three of us, created by our collective past history and filled with biological myths. This psychic field of hatred rendered the server incapable of acknowledging the lives before her. She was unable to directly experience us, or to recognize the multiplicity of sacred life. A particular thought and image of who we were worked in her like a numbing potion, enabling her act of overlooking us. The thoughts and images inherited from history or media sustained and validated her choice to overlook our lives.

It's a game that deletes people from the world even as they stand before you. We play it among ourselves when we cannot bear to include in our worlds people who we wish did not exist. The mental game of hatred is injurious to the wellness of all living beings. The inability to acknowledge all life in its multiplicity as it presents itself leads us down murky alleys—which for some of us may not be metaphorical—to be assaulted, violated, or murdered. Might we transform our capacity to annihilate others with a distant, ignoring stare into a liberated tenderness wherein knowledge of the sacredness of life prevails despite the continued presence of hatred? Might our woundedness be transformed from a persistent soreness into liberated tenderness?

Could my beloved and I have a raw, sore tenderness and be well? Yes, if we could arouse a complete tenderness that recognizes and acknowledges life's distortions. If we could experience the server as one who harbors a distorted view, even though we were the ones who felt the pain, we would be less likely to feel victim to the server, and less likely to want to hurt her in the way we felt hurt before we met her. We would then be able to nod to the experience and not be taken aback by it. If we recognized the server as part of the multiplicity of oneness, there would have been room for her and us, however painful. She would not be annihilated and neither would we. We do not have to make room for her hatred, but by acknowledging our lives in the realm of oneness we would acknowledge her life as well. If I would have responded verbally, in pain, I would have lost a chance to heal and she would have been affirmed in her actions. If I were to respond to all the rejection I experience daily I would go mad—and believe me some folks like me have.

⋯✄ **If we can recognize the multiplicity of life in one-ness, even in the midst of distraction, distortion, and harmful discrimination, we can effectively enter into a collective affirmation of all life, even when complete justice and wellness are lacking.** We still make the vow to end all suffering and to produce complete justice and wellness. When we recognize the multiplicity of life in oneness, our spiritual path or social activism does not become a means to an end, is not misused or hijacked by the need to escape from the horrors of the world or to justify the same.

When we see multiplicity as the varied expressions of nature we are better able to understand that all living beings on this planet exist within oneness. To say that all living beings exist within inherent oneness is to say more than "we are all one" or that "we are all in this troubled world together." It isn't as if we are all different but contained inside some larger encompass-ing vessel. We are not like passengers inside a leaky boat. Oneness existed before us and before the troubled world. Nothing can leak into or submerge oneness. It can't be possessed—it is not "our" oneness. Seeing the multiplicity of oneness means to acknowledge that there is an innate nonhistorical experience of oneness that we have no control over. It is ungraspable. We are not one. Oneness is itself and we are within it.

When we try to manipulate the nature of our oneness into a flat, one-dimensional sameness, we choose to ignore the concurrent multiplicity of nature. The sameness of being one does not erase difference. We need not make a union of sameness and difference, for they are already perfect—two aspects of the single dynamic relationship that is the nature of life. When we look out onto a garden and see curly willow trees, roses, succulents, collard greens, and plum blossoms, we are witnessing oneness. We don't have the power to create it.

Experiencing oneness requires that we drop any idea of it. When we have an idea of oneness we tend to pursue it, to attempt to make use of it, or to experience the pain of our lives in relation to our superficial idea of it. We may end up seeing oneness simply as a "we-ness," in the sense that "we are all one," that we are "peopled" together. We-ness is not reliable. Our worlds are cracked open when we discover that for many we are not part of the "we," because our differences are unacceptable differences to them. I clearly remember those moments when any sense of "we" cracked and shattered because I was deemed unacceptable. Just as we have to ask ourselves "Who am I?" we must ask ourselves who this "we" is. It is not enough to exchange the delusion "I" for another, more appealing delusion called "we." We must not perpetuate a false sense of oneness. There is no need to work at oneness. It already exists in nature. Eventually, we have to come home to ourselves, to see clearly our original face, unborn to suffering, in the natural garden of oneness.

Acknowledging the existence of varied embodiments in our lives does not negate oneness. If doing so could take oneness away, then what kind of oneness would that be? What kind of oneness has exclusion as part of it?

⋅⋅➢ **What about the type of "exclusion" within spiritual communities that happens when those who need cultural sanctuaries create them?** What about the need to create an exclusive space for people of color, queer folks, women, or others? What about the *appearance* of not being inclusive of everything and everyone? Are these cultural sanctuaries not the same as the exclusionary practices that have harmed people in this country?

A young man of mixed ethnicity came to speak with me after I led a people of color meditation session and discussion group. His white friends were upset that they couldn't come with him to the people of color group. He felt guilty about being there.

I asked him a few questions: "Do you feel that your friends do not have access to the Dharma? Are they being given inferior teachings in other places? Does it feel as though the people of color group exists to enforce the superiority of colored folks and render whiteness inferior for the sake of dominance?"

He shook his head "no" to all three questions.

"We all share the same oneness," I told him. "We

are all in the same garden, but in different parts of it. Some plants need light and some need shade. Some are dying and some are not. We are in different parts of the garden because it is necessary."

For everyone to thrive equally, we must meet the unique needs of each group.

Where and how do we meet the issues unique to people of color? Some may assume that there are no differences between people of color, that people of color share the same exact life experience. But even within the communities that we share by virtue of color there exist tensions and polarization of its own making. So I must ask those who attend people of color groups how we can avoid falling into the familiar spiritual stupor of "we are all one" without addressing the suffering among us. We must also explore the ways in which we may have internalized the sense of superiority and inferiority that pervades our society at large. We must ask ourselves, "Is there unconscious disdain among people of color?" and, "What does our use of the words 'people of color' imply?"

As blogger Janani writes of her own experience in the Black Girl Dangerous blog, "even if Black and Asian kids had a common experience of being racialized, we didn't have a common racialized experience."[3] We, as people of color, have specific spiritual work to contend with, and the term "people of color" suggests that work rather than the idea of separation based on skin color for the sake of harming those who are "white."

{ 57 }

I have written of this in my essay "Bearing Up in the Wild Winds":

> What is the suffering often felt by people of color? There is no one answer. But I suspect that we have been taught to love everyone and then have felt betrayed and angered when that love was not returned. We have been deeply wounded by this betrayal and have searched out ways to recover the loving people that we know ourselves to be. We have created names for ourselves, such as "people of color," in order to label the pain. We have created sanctuaries to heal and still have yet to emerge for those sanctuaries for fear of being hurt once again. What happens to a hurt people? We forget that we are butterflies bearing up in the wild winds. We forget that we are tender from the suffering.[4]

Although many of us emerge from cultural sanctuaries from time to time, emerging is not our focus or what's important about their existence. Each ethnic group has a unique history and impact of that history to contend with: the destruction of indigenous peoples and their lands, being targets of immigration laws, labor abuse in sweatshops and on farms, disproportionately high rates of imprisonment, or being the only group of people who were enslaved on this continent.

These unique historical conditions are at the root of all of our spiritual paths. Creating and entering sanctuaries allows us as people of color to address the circumstances that are specific to who we have been born as, on our own terms, without interference. The desire of those who are not people of color to enter the spaces where people of color face these issues betrays a disregard for the uniqueness of the work that must be done within these cultural sanctuaries. It indicates an unjust sense of entitlement on their part.

••❧ I have heard cultural sanctuaries likened to Jim Crow discrimination. Those who say such things argue that cultural sanctuaries within the larger spiritual community are counter to oneness and are places of exclusion. The root of this line of thought is the notion that the tables have turned, that the creation of exclusive sanctuaries for people of color are a sign that we have reverted to a past history of discrimination in this country. So we might ask ourselves, "What difference is there between the Jim Crow laws of our past and the creation of separate sanctuaries?"

Jim Crow laws were mandates from 1876 to 1965 in the United States in southern and northern regions where black-skinned people were segregated by law (*de jure*) in the South and in practice (*de facto*) in the North. This legal and practical discrimination was meant to ensure the social and political superiority of whites and the inferiority of blacks. Because of such laws, blacks did not have access to quality food, education, or housing, which furthered the illusion that black people were inferior and white ones superior. Of course, this is an extremely simplified description of a period in our national history wherein a great many suffered legal and practical discrimination. And many still suffer today because our national psyche still holds the notion of inferior and superior human beings that was systematically embedded there during Jim Crow days.

I briefly review the horrendous nature of what has been the lived experience for many of us in order to show that appeals to the legacy of Jim Crow to dispute the appropriateness of having cultural sanctuaries within spiritual communities are a misuse of history. Creating communities within communities based on uniquely shared experience of having been systematically discriminated against is not a turning of the tables from the Jim Crow laws of our past. White-skinned people or heterosexual people are not being rendered legally and practically inferior, and thereby losing access to the teachings, receiving inferior teachings, or being shut out of the community in which the teachings are shared. By gathering in sanctuary, people of color or queer people are not ensuring their superiority nor ensuring the inferiority of others. When they separate and create a sanctuary, people of color are not reducing the quality of white people's lives in any way.

To the contrary, in sanctuaries based on culture we attend to the impact that existing notions of inferior and superior human beings has had on us, and work at healing ourselves. Our healing does not have a deadline. The sanctuaries help us to voice and heal the suffering we have endured because of the misinterpretations and misconceptions based on our particular embodiments. We share this in common because our bodies, with unacceptable differences that set them apart, are the very foundation of the personal and systematic oppression within our society. To enter a sanctuary of healing is the way of tenderness—a way to provide needed compassion, perhaps a tender response to those entering an unfamiliar spiritual path. Sanctuaries based on love, rather than hatred, of others cannot harm anyone.

It has been my experience that in many predominantly white spiritual communities people of color are expected to "graduate" from being concerned with issues of race after having learned and put into practice all that has been taught, while others are considered to have an almost inherent understanding of the teachings related to identity and the self that does not require a similar "graduation." To speak of race, sexuality, and gender seems to be widely considered a reversion to a primitive, infantile place on the spiritual path. I would like to suggest, however, that to view cultural sanctuaries as oneness is an experience of tenderness.

It demonstrates a willingness to acknowledge the rifts of our living together and to consider healing them. When we acknowledge both the sanctuaries and the larger community as symbiotic, as part of the common spiritual landscape, we experience the true essence of oneness in practice.

Nothing can be taken away from our oneness because nothing can be extracted from the dynamic of nature, from the source of which we are born.

••❯ In his *Sandokai*, Zen master Sekito Kisen poetically speaks of how the oneness and the multiplicity of things coexist. He eloquently writes:

> Trunk and branches share the essence;
> revered and common, each has its speech.

The one trunk shares the essence of being a tree, yet the trunk has its oneness and relationship with multiple roots, and the branches are multiple while having a relationship with the one trunk. "Each has its own speech" points to its multiplicity in the oneness. In the *Jewel Mirror Samadhi*, Ch'an Master Dongshan Liangjie writes:

> Filling a silver bowl with snow, hiding a heron
>   in the moonlight.
> Taken as similar they're not the same; when you
>   mix them, you know where they are.

This perfectly describes the experience of harmonizing. Nothing is lost.

When we have an idea of harmony without an understanding that difference exists within oneness, we end up creating separation between people. Alternately, multiplicity may be mistaken for perceiving individual things one at a time, for perceiving each thing as separate, or for being excluded from oneness. When we see things strictly through the lens of separation we may think that we can hate someone without hating ourselves. From the point of view of oneness it is impossible to truly love while hating anyone else.

Race, sexuality, and gender are collective manifestations. Rarely do we consider these collective manifestations to be such when we enter the room to reveal, acknowledge, and heal them. We see them as individual points of view on life. Acknowledging that we are in fact interrelated, even within constructed (or delusional) categories of our unique embodiment, is a significant part of shifting the old dialogue. Being able to see that race, gender, and sexuality encompass everyone is at the core of the transformation of consciousness, and of our interactions with each other.

At the same time seeing race, sexuality, and gender as encompassing everyone can be confusing. We are confused by the idea of multiplicity in oneness because of the word "one." If we are "one," how can we be "different"? Language fails to express what is truly inexpressible. There really is no need to linguistically define this when we can experience it directly in life. The natural state of confusion that comes with holding ideas of shared humanity alongside ideas of intrinsic differences in terms of race, gender, and sexuality shakes up our sense of certainty about who we are. This type of confusion provides an opportunity to find profound meaning within the very conditions of our lives, rather than finding it artificially in books or secondhand through another's experience. When confronted with confusion, we are more likely to look deeply into how we observe each other and ourselves. When shifted off of our usual, comfortable platforms (whatever they might be), a deep and curious sense of inquiry emerges that doesn't occur when we feel settled and certain.

We may wonder about many things: Does our way of seeing difference come only from being enmeshed in the political arena, from having had to fight, justly, for our survival? Are those who haven't had to fight like we have somehow removed from the realm of difference? Do they have some special claim to the experience of oneness? Given that difference itself is not suffering, what causes us to suffer so in relation to our difference? Can we approach each other without an immediate desire for oneness or harmony?

··⊱ We all run up against social borders in our lives that can seem as wide as oceans, or as narrow as creeks.

Eventually we are compelled to cross into unknown territory, to venture onto dangerous or forbidden ground. Yet the most difficult borders to cross are the ones within ourselves—the ones we can't touch but which we certainly feel.

For fifteen years prior to taking up the practice of Zen I had been studying Buddha's teachings with the Soka Gakkai, a lay organization, centered on the teachings of Nichiren Daishonin.[5] I practiced devotion and concentration largely with practitioners who were much like me in terms of their embodiment and lived experience. Together with them I learned the power of chanting and how rhythm can change the course of one's life. Still, even with such power at hand, my inability to face suffering persisted. The process of attending to such suffering with chanting was not enough for me.

When the gateway to Zen opened I wasn't seeking it. I had no particular desire to understand Zen. At first I was resistant to teachings of emptiness, no self, or impermanence with regard to the felt presence of hatred in my life. Zen practice seemed to me to be an individual practice that paid no attention to socially imposed suffering. So when I did come to Zen practice I needed something to bridge the gap between where I stood in my life and the Zen teachings being espoused. Despite my inability to immediately embrace the teachings, the constant pull toward liberation and the urge to ease suffering demanded that I stay and see what the Zen perspective really had to offer.

At the beginning, I joined a people of color Zen group. I had a sanctuary in which to share my experience and where I could cry when needed without having to deal with the unfamiliar world of the Zen center. From the sanctuary of the people of color group I could contemplate whether I was ready for the stripping down of beliefs that Zen requires on the path of liberation. I slowly developed trust in Dogen's basic Zen teaching: To study the Buddha Way is to study the self. To study the self is to forget the self. To forget the self is to be enlightened by the ten thousand things.

When I first heard this teaching I did not want to forget about being who I was or about my collective identity as an African American. At the time, I felt that "to forget the self" meant to let myself disappear without a trace. I was concerned about what this would mean to my life given the suffering I had endured living in a dark-skinned body. Was I to forget the suffering as well? Later I learned that when Dogen said "forget the self," he didn't mean to render ourselves unconscious or develop an acute case of amnesia, but rather to untangle ourselves from what we believed was "real" about ourselves and the world around us. What was real or unreal about blackness? This was a spiritual question for me as I began to walk the path in the people of color sanctuary.

Before long I wanted to learn Zen rituals, chants, and attend the long *sesshins* (seven-day sittings). Those activities took place as a part of the larger Sangha, which was predominantly white. If I wanted to follow my interests, it felt as though I would have to cross over the water from the people of color group to the Sangha at large. Sometimes we have to leave the comfort of home, as the Buddha did, in order to discover truth. Truth often emerges through discomfort. I felt ready to test the waters of Zen that seemed cold from my vantage point in the people of color Sangha. In those cold waters I would have to investigate the ideas I relied upon.

Finally, I left the shelter of the people of color group and crossed the water. The suffering I perceived on the planet and my intense wish to save my own life drove me to study, to train, and to practice as a spiritual warrior despite perceived discomfort. To begin, I needed to work with my own rage and fear of whiteness. However, it was only when I crossed that I found just how deep was the fissure beneath the water that separated me from the Zen Sangha at large. I felt that I was held suspect for having been in a group *for* people of color, that somehow that sanctuary was a form of "reverse" racism. Despite feeling this way I could not turn back from the call to deepen my Zen practice. Having left the sanctuary behind, I was exposed, naked. I felt that I had nothing solid to hold on to in those waters. I didn't know how to swim in the Zen world, so I said to myself, "Watch and see who you are here."

For years I had floated in the world of Zen, acknowledging both the body I was born to and the practice that called me, a practice that taught that all this is empty, that there is no individual life standing apart from all others. Eventually, I swam into the arms of a few compassionate Zen teachers. I sat for years in the zendo where, wordlessly, an awareness of multiplicity in oneness and of the body as nature dawned in me. I began to see that what I wanted from others, despite the color of their skin, was love. I wanted to be looked upon with undeniable love. I wanted the acceptance, the connectedness that I knew in my bones existed between living beings. I wanted respect for being human. I wanted this from the people of color Sangha, the larger Sangha, and the world at large. This haunting desire came from suffering the loss of connectedness in the face of experiences of systemic oppression. I had not forgotten the connectedness we come into the world with when we are born. Knowledge of our inherent interrelationship as beings still lay deep in my bones, despite the suffering I had experienced.

Why did I stay in such a white, male dominated spiritual community? Because by turning away from wanting what I already knew and had, I came to see and hear myself better. It became clear that engaging white male dominance was not my work, even though it impacted me. My practice was to engage Zenju Earthlyn Marselean Manuel, to stand her up on her two feet, and trust that facing what hurt the most was a great enough response to the human condition within and around me. I could see that I no longer needed love or acceptance from others. These experiences were not in the hands of others but already available to me. Confronting racism, sexism, homophobia, slavery, and genocide as a whole inside a community would have furthered my rage and taken me away from the healing that my soul cried out for. I was not willing to act as a barometer for oppression while others walked away with the teachings. I remained on the path of Dharma, preserving my energy for those few moments when silence would have been harmful to everyone.

My practice never would have been possible without the sheltering cradle of the people of color group.

••❧ **Consciousness of multiplicity in oneness let me allow people to be who they were, without any expectations.** It isn't that I experienced no pain or suffering to get to that point. Like many, I have been hurt and disappointed by spiritual places and people. The difference is that I stopped taking it upon myself to change them. I did speak up and consult others when necessary, but I retained what I knew in my bones—that awareness of oneness in life includes difference. In the end, I realized that conflict only appears when I see the people of color group and the larger Sangha as contradictory to one another; conflict appears if I fail to recognize that the practice of compassion is still necessary no matter which part of the garden I am planted in. Others would have to simply recognize for themselves the entire landscape of living beings.

Cultural sanctuaries help shape paths according to a specific life experience. Paths like the path of Dharma are shaped by the cultures into which they are adopted. The Pure Land Buddhism of China is different than the Thai forest tradition of Buddhism and the Zen Buddhism of Japan is different than the Zen Buddhism of Korea or Vietnam. When Buddhism first came out of Asia, it was shaped by white men of European descent who were taught by Asian men. Asian teachers taught their European and American students and allowed them to shape Dharma paths of their own. All throughout the world, the teachings are shaped by those who take them on.

Our potent contemporary cultural sanctuaries shape the Dharma to fit our cultural traditions so that the mirroring needed for spiritual paths to work can occur. It is important to the viability of any path that students see themselves reflected in it. This does not have to be only in terms of race, sexuality, or gender, but also in terms of the true nature of students' lives. Such mirroring happens in the Sangha. This is why people of color often feel that Zen centers and other Buddhist centers are not places meant for them: we often do not see ourselves or the true nature of our lives reflected there.

The Buddha's teachings that are passed on in Dharma centers can certainly benefit everyone. But we will not recognize our true nature until we honestly look at ourselves. To embark on that path of healing or liberation requires exposure—where we can be comfortably seen without encountering another's guilt, explanation, or justification. We have the opportunity within cultural sanctuaries to experience interrelationship without otherizing expectations of how we should behave. If the group is facilitated by a mature and wise teacher, a complete exploration of life as relative *and* absolute, as tangible *and* intangible, material *and* spirit, becomes possible. We come to the path that eases our suffering by having a complete view of suffering rather than a view of life based on appearances alone.

Cultural sanctuaries provide a space where appearance doesn't act as a platform to launch diversity campaigns, or provide a basis for special attention, which many people of color do not want. They are refuges in which one can participate in the collective, rather than being perceived as a distinct individual in the midst of sameness. Cultural sanctuaries are created within spiritual and sociopolitical spaces to offer an alternate entrance to practice such that those who pass its threshold can experience the liberated tenderness available to them. Cultural sanctuaries are not meant only to diversify an institution, although that might be an outcome. In the face of our consciousness of multiplicity, cultural sanctuaries are the varied expression of oneness.

••❥ **Oneness is not harmony; oneness is itself, harmony is itself.** We are quick to name harmony or what is harmonious based on our own particular views. We might say harmony is when you feel happy. Harmony is when people are all getting along together. Harmony is when people are nice to one another or harmony is the flow of life. So we go about trying to be happy, to get along, to be nice, to flow like a river, or to force our environment to be one in which everyone agrees. But really, if we look deeper, we are uncertain of harmony. We want to apply the idea of harmony to our various spiritual paths, hoping that it will mean that we will make a harmonic sound together as people.

In my churchgoing days the entire congregation sang *a capella* on Sundays. Because it was a fundamentalist church, they believed that singing with instruments obscured the offering of our pure voices to Christ. The entire church would sing in four-part harmony: soprano, alto, tenor, and bass. If we had a good song leader our voices would sound like the chords of any musical instrument, crescendos and all. I sang alto alongside my oldest sister. As the songs gathered momentum I would shiver every time. Goose bumps. I still experience this chill today when a song or chant touches some place inside my body that my mind cannot name. I have felt this chill while dancing and even when sitting silently. The chill rises up in the body on its own; I have nothing to do with it.

Harmony, like the chill, reveals itself. We need a body in which it can be revealed. Harmony is seen, heard, and felt with the body. It resides in the body and it is only through the body that we experience harmony. Thus, harmony may be seen as an expression of the body, of nature. It expresses itself without our doing. We have nothing to do with the fragrance of harmony. Like the fragrance that emanates from rosemary, it simply wafts up into the air and surrounds us.

Given this, we need not insist that discussions of race, sexuality, and gender adversely affect the appearance of harmony or cause it to disappear. The notion that acknowledging lived experience is misaligned with spirituality is something we've made up in our minds, and not the natural reality of things. We must study the self in order to discover harmony in our own lives. We must listen to the earth right under our feet no matter what. We must constantly be attuned to the unfolding of life as it presents the multitude of variations in which harmony manifests in nature as oneness.

We cannot ignore the constructs that have emerged in our lives as they unfold in each moment or ignore the manifold ways in which suffering is experienced. As the teacher Mooji-ji says, "We suffer our experiences; it is not that our experience of life *is* suffering." We can live our experiences open-handed, unburdened, empty of imposing things upon our forms, upon our hearts.

If we carry awareness of the body as our inheritance of nature, as tender as a maple leaf or a small hummingbird, then the experience of complete tenderness can rise and swell within our ever-evolving relative reality.

We will evolve beyond running from or tracking down monsters, to communicating on all levels of awareness, even that which goes beyond the body. We must begin with the body and acceptance of it as nature.

Body as Nature

—— ··❧ ❧·· ——

My mother and I stood on the porch steps—barefooted two-tones of brown, against the red cement. Everyone else's steps on the block west of Main St. in Los Angeles were red like ours. My father's prized possession of St. Augustine grass stood blue green, thick, and tough a few feet ahead. That day the wind had a smell, turpentine. Yes, like someone had been rubbing down a fever. The little girl up the street died and that was the smell that came to me on the wind.

My mother whispered to a neighbor that the poor little thing had died, as if I were not standing there. What thing?

"You mean Valerie," I said, my tongue filling in the spaces where my front teeth used to be.

Mom looked at me; her eyes were sad even though she didn't really know Valerie. I didn't know her well either, only played with her a few times.

Mom said she had asked for milk and honey before she died. *Milk and honey?* I thought, *Why not a donut, vanilla ice cream, or sweet potato pie?* That she had asked for milk and honey meant she was going to heaven, the neighbor said. She went on talking about how Valerie had been sick for a while, wasn't getting better, and that her aunt from Louisiana was too poor to take good care of her.

"We're all going to die," my mother said. There was no fear in her voice.

I t was Valerie's death that sparked questions for me about living and suffering. The pumping of my heart felt different. I was perishable. My parents could not save me. That day I embarked on a lifetime quest to grasp the reality of this body. What is this body? Why is this color, this shape hated by some and loved by others? My very first Dharma questions in life were given to the suffering I experienced as a black girl child.

The French philosopher Maurice Merleau-Ponty said, "We know not through our intellect but through our experience." We perceive the world through our bodies. If the world of perception resides within the body, then the path of spirituality or Dharma must include the body. The path must include the facts of our being raced, gendered, and sexualized sentient beings.

George Yancy, an African American philosopher

and author of *Black Bodies, White Gazes*, reminds us that our bodies are socially constituted within a lived history and a lived experience. This lived experience shapes the question of a spiritual path. In my case, for example, questions about oppression, trauma, and identity within the racist, sexist, and homophobic contexts have shaped the particular path of my life as I walk it. At the same time this lived experience is mutable and is shifting because diverse ways of living constantly multiply and perspectives change. In other words, our bodies are not strictly objective: we are ever-evolving sentient beings. No matter how hard we try, assuming objectivity with regard to our embodiment is a transient mental process and is impacted by impermanence.

From the first pages of this book I have been aware that my own embodiment brings a specific subjectivity to the topics I discuss. I don't truly know the experiences of others who are differently embodied than I am— black men, white people, and so on. I have some experience, however, trying to adopt a white male mindset in order to succeed in institutions dominated by white men. I also have experienced living as a heterosexual. It is important for me to name this ever-evolving subjectivity as I focus on the notion of liberation. This focus provides a ground on which to explore the liberation that comes from the body, from the heart, which is not just some idea of liberation.

There are many possible meanings or experiences of spiritual liberation as it emerges from within. I experience it as freedom from projections of superiority and inferiority among sentient beings. To experience liberation in such a way is to experience authentic compassion, wisdom, love, and interrelationship. Authentic experiences of these qualities do not come with ideas that someone is better or worse than anyone else. Liberation comes from within the body when we clearly see, not only with our eyes but with our hearts, who and what has erroneously claimed power and domination over others in this life; it is when we clearly see the dominance of one over others as fear and hatred manifested in action. Liberation from within affects both the personal bodies and the collective body of living beings; it has both personal and social dimensions.

In addition, liberation within the body encompasses the notion that our bodies are the places through which we make meaning of our lives. In order to fully explore and experience liberation from within it is crucial to understand that our bodies are not only biological but are "lived sites of meaning," as famed French/Martinique-Algerian philosopher Frantz Fanon said many years ago. We live within our bodies and therefore perceive life through them. When violence is gendered we see the meaning of lives through such violence. When terror is racialized, particularly against black male bodies, young black males see the meaning of their lives through that terror. When a man rapes a lesbian to "cure" her, she sees the meaning of her experience of her life through such threats of annihilation. Religious or biological approaches to such tragedies that are purely theoretical overlook the palpable dimensions of racialized, sexualized, and gendered experience that shape the meaning of life for many. If we consider a spiritual path as a path through which we live out our lives, then we must bring our lived experiences along with us as we walk it.

·•❧ When I set out on the path of Dharma, the question of what this life was dealt squarely with my immediate physical reality, meaning, in my case, my race, sexuality, and gender. I was not out to rendezvous with abstract philosophical ideas (although I love them) but was posing a deep and complex inquiry into suffering and enchantment. I walked with questions about life in relationship to the suffering I endured. I used what I had enjoyed and what I had suffered to understand life.

I found that if I allowed myself to be held hostage by suffering, or by joy for that matter, I would overlook awakening and fail to experience or live it. To awaken I acknowledged the pain, but not just for the sake of expressing it emotionally, although that is fine. To acknowledge our pain is to recognize the complexity of our bodies as both the place in which we forge meaning for our lives, and the location within which we catalyze liberation. When we are aware of pain, we can say, "Ah, this hurts. I have finally been touched after having been numb for so long." We can discover tenderness and use it as the wellspring from which to draw as we seek liberation. We can allow that which we have suffered to be a moment of our lives, but not our whole lives. We can see what is truly in our own hearts. We feel, we breathe, and we can still say it hurts. We are complex: we are not just filled with pain and rage but with well-being. Our experiences of rage and well-being exist alongside each other. On the path of awakening we attend to both.

Sobonfu Somé, healer and keeper of Dagara African wisdom, says that to feel suicidal is at least to feel something. It is better than a state of numbness, where no healing can enter. When emotional pain arises and we know it as something that passes, we can attend to the emotion rather than end our lives. We have simply forgotten how to attend to our emotions. Somé says that we experience loss everyday. We often have no words for that loss, and because our lives are so busy we may not even know that we are grieving it. If we don't grieve we won't get healthy. The body has to recover from loss in order for us to experience safety and sanity. I will go one step further and say that grieving what we have lost of ourselves specifically with regard to race, sexuality, and gender is also critical to our wellness. In continually judging, mistreating, and hating we have lost sight of the basic connectedness we were born with. When will we grieve it?

We have the capacity to see our subjectivity, to see

our embodiment as useful to the spiritual path, to see our embodiment as creating meaning for our lives, and to see it as the location of awakening. To seriously consider the ways in which our spiritual paths are shaped by our multiple identities and subjectivities is the way of tenderness. To awaken from within our unique embodiment is to awaken collective awareness: spiritual awakening and social activism are one and the same.

Liberation cannot be experienced through introspection alone or while waiting for others to point out places of oppression. It is not won solely in deep exploration or by simply seeing racism, sexism, or homophobia in the closed quarters of abstract study. We must, all of us, openly acknowledge the real norms, desires, biological myths, and practices that fuel racial, sexual, and gender-based hatred. Our collective liberation requires that society, which is a collective body, turn within to face and dissolve the hatred that has claimed our lives. Society, as the collective body, must reconcile the harm within and without. It must say, "Ah, we have willingly hurt ourselves and other people. We have covered up our mess for so long." Society must learn to see. A society that does not examine itself is an unenlightened one.

We cannot be an enlightened society without facing ourselves. A society that survives examines itself. It aligns its own internal beliefs of peace and wellness with its external actions. Society can't change itself by seeking relief elsewhere. By seeking elsewhere we lose the opportunity to witness ourselves as a society. We lose a chance to meaningfully transform the fear and oppression we impose on each other. Our essential human nature as peace, truth, awareness, and love will be lost if we fail to look to ourselves. We should not exalt our rage over our pain out of fear of losing strength and momentum. If we do so, we are likely to justify violence in order to maintain our strength. At the same time, being frightened of our rage and allowing ourselves to feel only our sadness is likely to lead to inner violence and a depressed society. No. We must fearlessly examine ourselves. A society that is fearful of self-examination and exploration can't believably say that it trusts in God. Nor can it believably say that it values every living being. We must trust the totality of our nature, in terms of both its multiplicity and its oneness.

A path that embraces the body as nature, that looks unflinchingly at the lived experiences that being differently embodied brings, enables us to envision a society that reclaims its power to see and listen clearly in order to go through the chaos of changing the familiar. Only by facing the reality of our unique subjectivities will we gain access to our humanly divine potential to truly eliminate hatred, without the need for protests or legislative acts, simply because we value every life. Such a path allows us to envision an end to war and poverty because they are counter to our wellness. Only when we fearlessly face up to ourselves will we be able to say it is time to mourn, to be still, and to rebuild our integrity as a people. Then we will ask ourselves, "What have we been taught?"

··҂ **What we see and hear about race, sexuality, and gender over our lives teaches us how to think about race, gender, and sexuality.** Without noticing it, we believe that what we have been taught about each other is true. When we began to recognize a distinction between what we have been taught and what we directly experience as true and authentic life, we begin to let go of erroneous images; we begin to see. If we are unaware of what we have stored in our consciousness with regard to race, sexuality, and gender, these unconscious inheritances begin to ripen as karmic tendencies. As they ripen we become subject to new forms of supremacy and oppression. What we have been taught shapes our actions, our karma. So far we have been taught to reinforce fear based on misperceptions of each other.

For example, one sunny afternoon as I was out for a walk I noticed a blonde, Nordic-looking woman and her blonde little girl coming my way. The little girl skipped blissfully down the pavement, enjoying the sun. When the mother saw me approaching, she called her daughter to come back to her. The child stopped skipping and the mother grabbed her arm. I can't say for sure what the mother was thinking, but it seemed as if she was trying to save her child from me. I wanted to let her know that she was making a mistake. I felt sad when the mother stopped her daughter from skipping, robbing all three of us of this beautiful display of happiness.

I smiled at the little girl despite my grief. She smiled back, and her mother said aloud, "Oh, she's friendly." It was as if I were potentially a rabid dog roaming the streets without its leash. Before they ran off, I wanted to say, "Hello," and let them know that I too was enjoying the sun (not to appease the mother or make her feel good but to share the beauty of oneness that we live in). Yes, even I, the dark African, walk in awareness of peace.

In *The Heart of the Buddha's Teachings*, Thich Nhat Hanh writes, "We are on the shore of suffering, anger, and depression, and we want to cross over to the shore of well-being." On that hill with the skipping child, my well-being depended on my ability to continue up the hill despite my sadness about what I felt to be the mother's fear. I could not wait around for my feelings to change about the mother or myself. I had to move forward with a liberated sense of what is inevitably our human condition. There is tension or friction in the movement of our lives based on our myths about each other. What is this tension that is diluted at times in spiritual settings?

••❧ Once I sat silently with a teacher during *dokusan*.[6] I was hesitant to discuss the details of what was going on with me so I was silent for a moment. I turned toward a window that I could not see out of, wishing for air. Finally, I began to speak of the problems in my life and of those I saw in the world that impacted my life. I didn't expect to hear any solutions. I just needed to talk. When I was done he smiled and said that life includes everything, even the "bad," and that I would not be alive if nothing was happening. He continued to point out that a desire for a life without problems was desire to live a life of fantasy. Life is filled with complicated situations and circumstances but in fact nonetheless perfect.

Perfect? What about the pain of being disregarded for how I appear in this world? Is he saying that the seemingly imperfect conflict and tension of life live right alongside perfect tranquility and freedom?

I had a similar experience with a relationship coach who said that an intimate relationship in which there was no struggle was a dead one. The coach said if we wanted to be liberated in the way the Dharma espouses, we would have to be in relationships that provide enough intimacy to create the friction needed for such liberation. In other words, she said relationships in which we seek only peace and quiet end up dying. I remembered being profoundly disappointed. I had been *struggling* to have a *struggle-free* life. This was not a perfect life.

Both teachers spurred me to look deeper at what I believed a perfect life to be. "Perfect" meant that everything was wonderful and all living beings were welcome. Perfect, to me, was a life without hunger, violence, hatred, illness, and disregard of human beings. Perfect was tied to someone or something making the world perfect so that I could live peacefully in it. We could even practice to become perfect if we so desired. So it was difficult for me to trust in the medicinal teaching that we must recognize friction and the not-so-good circumstances in life as being life, and that this life is perfect. It was hard to trust, swallow, and keep down this medicine, especially in conjunction with the hatred I had experienced and internalized for most of my life. I gagged on this teaching of the perfect life, as I have seen many others do. It is perfect because it is imperfect.

I suspect that Buddha did not see old age, sickness, and death as perfect on his first journey out of the palace either. What he saw made him sit down on the earth. He contemplated what did not appear perfect in comparison to his princely life. That inquiry led to his teaching of compassion and wisdom based on the suffering he witnessed. I suspect that when he had deeply contemplated old age, sickness, and death, he no longer felt himself to be distinct from those lying about in the streets—the old, the infirm, the pariahs.

Buddha came to see that he could not separate himself from others with thoughts of superiority, even though it was difficult for him to see women as fit and capable followers in his times (even today, many traditions forbid the ordination of women). By sitting with the teaching that this life, every aspect of it, is the perfect life, I came to understand the depth of the waters of compassion. Without understanding these deep waters we cannot see perfection as everything we experience as human beings.

··⸙·A simplistic understanding of compassion as being aware of other's situations and feeling sympathy because of it can be a hindrance to fully accessing the medicine of compassion. When I grew still enough with all that I suffered, I came to recognize that to walk the path of compassion and wisdom is to carry no *harmful* distinctions within our personal lives or between ourselves and others. Distinctions exist, and there are times when discrimination is needed, but need we make harmful distinctions? Harmful distinctions are what render other living beings expendable in our minds. As I experienced being disregarded, I learned to disregard others. The experience grew into a symbiotic cycle of disrespect and dehumanization. We learn to pass our suffering on to others. When we are in a position of dominance, we are able to pass the suffering on with prolonged and cruel mistreatment of groups of people. This is what is called "systemic oppression"—it is internalized by the dominated and externalized by the dominator.

A world that systematically disregards specific

people is not only experienced on a personal level but indicates that there is a collective mental state that makes harmful distinctions rooted in our society. This collective mental state seeps into all of our social environments, including temples and other spiritual or sacred sanctuaries. The presence of this pervasive mental state is what makes it a struggle to maintain dignity, respect, and honor.

As a sexually free human being who happens to love across normative gender divides, I recognize that the deep history of supremacy in our country undermines the natural interrelationship among living beings. The asymmetrical representation of white, wealthy, male, heterosexual supremacy as *the* image of embodiment everywhere and in everything in our society perpetuates the false notion that a single group of people depends upon others, rather than reflecting the true nature of life as the mutual interdependence of all. Once we understand the power of false and harmful distinctions (superior and inferior) and the ever-increasing tension that it can produce, we can understand the selective, differential prevalence of the dis-ease of hypertension with regard to race, sexuality, and gender. The disparity caused by harmful distinctions manifests itself physically in those of us who are deemed inferior. So I had to learn to breathe deeply if I were going to stay alive. If I were going to avoid the health trajectory toward hypertension, diabetes, and congenital heart and/or kidney failure that are more common among people like myself, I would have to unearth the internalized lessons we had been taught and stored within ourselves on what and who is superior or inferior. What kind of world would we live in if we don't develop the wisdom to let go of the mindset of hatred for the sake of our own well-being?

Images and biological myths have been enacted and enforced to sustain a false dominance by those deemed "superior." There is nothing more dominant than the true nature of life. Our bodies, physically and spiritually, are a part of that very nature. Therefore, awakening to the challenges of race, sexuality, and gender begins in the body, where we struggle. Awakening means to open our hearts wide enough to encompass the perfection within this tension as a part of our path, rather than crashing against the hardness of our inevitable differences. If we are struggling, are we ready to let go of what we have been taught?

Charles Johnson, novelist and Buddhist scholar, wrote to me in a correspondence: "I believe the heart of the matter is the necessity of freeing ourselves from presuppositions, judgments about beings, and freeing ourselves from *māna* (pride)." He asks that we consider an "epistemological humility and thanksgiving in the presence of others." He calls for investigating what we think we know: imagine a thanksgiving every time you encounter a living being. Are we ready to reassess our loyalties, our borders, our pasts, and our conditioned responses to each other? When we pause in our interactions through body, speech, and mind, are we ready to consider how we see each other in truth? Can we honestly examine our thinking and our habits?

When we take inventory of our actions and inquire whether they are timely, helpful, necessary, true, or kind, as Buddha recommends in the Araṅavibhanga Sutta, we are not simply trying to be nice to everyone or to modify our behavior so as to appear kind in order to relieve social tension. With such inquiry we put some distance between our past experiences and the present, so we can see what is happening in this moment. We are more likely to feel an inner bow toward others—or "a thanksgiving," as Charles Johnson says—when this gap between past and present experience is available, even when the friction in our encounters are triggered by how we appear to each other.

What is this friction? How have we inherited this situation? Do our personal views of ourselves blind us to our true inheritance? We may think that our inheritance is only the money and property that is handed down to us, but it is not. We have already received our inheritance. What did we inherit? We inherited *nature* the moment we were born. The moment we came into existence, we entered the landscape of nature. In fact we are nature. Nature is form. Body is form. Body is nature. Nature is body.

•◦► **Seeing body as nature is to directly see form as nature, as of the earth.** It is to see the pure form of life without the distortions. Although we are confronted with the challenge of the varied forms of nature, we have a tendency to view this challenge as strictly non-organic, as not of nature. Rage springs up when certain embodied forms of life—blackness, queerness, and so on—are not recognized and honored as part of nature. The embodiments of race, sexuality, and gender are in fact the fires through which we must pass to awaken. The fire will not destroy us if we can see authentic inter-relationship in its flames.

Are these bodies really the enemy of the spirit? Do our struggles with race, sexuality, and gender belie a hidden denial of the body, a mortification of the flesh? Need we sacrifice our bodies in the name of spiritual attainment—hurting our backs and knees far too long in meditation? Why do we ignore the nature of our bodies, something we all share in common? What is this body?

Where there is a dead body, it is said, there too do the vultures gather.

When my father died I sat listening to the minister at his funeral. Mom and I sat next to each other. Neither one of us was crying. I was surprised to see that my own reaction was stoic, like hers. I leaned over, "Mom, you don't like to cry in public do you?"

She leaned back, "No, I do all my crying at night in private."

"Me too," I said, "Me too." I sat back viewing my father's body dressed in a black Armani tuxedo, something he never could have afforded during his life. I don't even know if this sharecropper's son knew what a tuxedo was.

He worked well into his eighties, only starting to raise his second family, the one to which I belonged, at the age of sixty. He sacrificed his aged body for us. His parents sacrificed theirs as enslaved children. His body, the body of my ancestry, had become more visible in death than it had been in life. Seeing my father's body made more visible to me the ways in which I had sacrificed my own body to cultivate my mind. In the past I had stayed too long in places where I was clearly being hurt, or I had just sat too long, worked past depletion, depriving my body of what it needed—health, good food, and rest.

To ignore our embodiment is not spiritual. How do we abuse these bodies, or hold them sacred, with respect to the challenges of race, sexuality, and gender? bell hooks once observed that the constant depiction of violence against women, black men, or queer folk in media implies an expectation of or permission for brutality against *and* between particular people off screen. We have stopped slaughtering animals so readily on film, but we stop short of doing the same with respect to people. But how do we investigate and transform such forms of hate?

We can't just legislate change, persuade others, or protest, without also transforming a hateful consciousness into one that is aligned with nature. In these chaotic times, amid disconnection, the kind of transformation needed is one in which we are aligned with our bodies, with the nature we inhabit. We must all first know that we have inherited nature. Our bodies are a form of nature; they should not to be hated, abused, or slaughtered. The body consists of all the great elements: earth, water, air, and fire. When we abuse collective social bodies we also abuse and pollute the collective elements. We ignore form as nature.

We humans have even gone to the moon and reached out to the stars and planets to see if other living forms of nature exists elsewhere than on our Earth. If they do, we have not seen them yet. So far, we can only be certain that living forms are earthly phenomena. Perhaps if we found similar forms elsewhere, we would more easily see the limits of our earthly distinctions and avoid racialized, sexualized, and gendered discriminations. We can acknowledge, as we walk our spiritual paths, that there are discoveries to be made about the nature of life. It is only due to these bodies in which we live that we can even explore the path to liberation. When we begin to hold an awareness of the body as inheriting nature, then we may begin to experience a liberating tenderness, to have authentic encounters, and to reconcile kinship between us.

•❥ **Everything we experience is because of the body.**
The body mediates our lives. We work to preserve the
body even though we know we will eventually lose it.
Our identities slip from one birth to the next. From
birth to birth we end up embodying humanity. Yet we
are often advised to let go of identifying with our personal embodiments for the sake of enlightenment.

In the face of such guidance, some find more reasons
to hold on to identity and others try to detach from the
body. Our personal experiences as straight people, as
brown people, as men, as women, as non-men, non-
women, may grow more intense. Or, on the detachment
end of the spectrum, we may become too aloof and lose
sight of everything and everyone around us. There is
still attachment to experience even in the act of being
aloof. When we detach we suppose there is something
to detach from. Who or what is it that is attached to
or detaches from embodiment? Identity is what we are
struggling with.

Pema Chödrön, Buddhist nun and teacher, says that
our embodied identities are fluid and dynamic. Our
incarnations in bodies are fixed but our identities are
as fluid as water. Unfortunately, we do not acknowledge this fluidity in our society. We don't typically see
a welfare mother as a potential corporate executive,
or a rich white man as a thug. The uncertainty about
identity that we hear about in spiritual communities
is not recognized in the world at large. If the fluidity
of identity were readily recognized, it would certainly

be more difficult to disenfranchise some or to privilege other groups of people. It would be much more difficult to monopolize resources in a society where identity is recognized as fluid. The truth is that we do not naturally see this fluidity. We all still think of ourselves and our identities in terms of our incarnated bodies, each with its own physical characteristics, even if these can be changed with modern technology or medical procedures.

When the natural fluidity of our identities erupts from within our ideas of who or what we are, the experience of the inevitable groundlessness of our selves is thrust upon us. In my experience, it is actually this groundlessness that we struggle with when we grow attached to or detach from the body and identification with it. Both acts revolve around the question, "Who or what am I?" In the process of building up or tearing down who or what we think we are, we come face to face with the unknown. Staring into this uncertainty, we quickly move to ground ourselves in some kind of identity or embrace the idea of erasing identity. The pull between grounding or erasing identity is the natural tension found on the spiritual path. Coming to see this natural tension allows us to see groundlessness or opening needed to experience liberation. We come to see evolution in such groundlessness.

According to Chödrön this groundlessness is the liberation within. The uncomfortable feeling of not having anything to grab on to is liberation. Likewise we cannot hold on to groundlessness to be liberated. An experience of groundlessness, nonclinging, is as impermanent as the body and the identity that goes with it. For this reason, seeking to be boundless when we are bound to the body can be a place of suffering in itself. It is difficult to not cling when we are embodied. The body is here until we die. This body is the path by which we experience the groundless nature of liberation.

Through experience with meditation over the years, it became clear to me that it would be impossible for me to completely drop identity as long as I was alive. When I witnessed my father's dead body I knew I would never completely achieve the dropping of body and mind or go beyond form and emptiness while I still breathed. Fortunately, I discovered moments of groundlessness in breathing. Who was I sitting on the cushion? There were moments of identity freed of clinging to what I knew myself to be. When the groundlessness passed I would return to the feeling of my body. Identity was still there. It was an identity integral to nature—if I lay dying in a desert, vultures would gather.

There is nothing wrong with identity in itself. Rather, the distortions—superior and inferior—that we place on it is what causes suffering. A tree is a tree. If we say a redwood is superior to an oak tree, we establish a different relationship with the oak than we do with the redwood. We might disregard oak trees and chop them down faster than we would redwoods. Identity is natural. If we can't completely drop identity, then how can we ease the suffering among us? We can begin by learning the difference between distorted identity and natural identity.

••❧ From a political perspective, we establish a sense of ourselves in relationship to the worlds we inhabit. Such relationships include constituted histories that are used to further biological myths or remind us of our indigenous beginnings. Our inherent natures are disembodied in the face of such identities, leaving us instead to embody the ways of society. M. Jacqui Alexander, author, priestess, and theorist of transnational feminism, points out that we inherit boundaries of geography, nation, ways of knowing, and identity that distort our vision. For some of us, she says, as a consequence of our historically having been brought across the sea from some other place, it became necessary that "we make the world intelligible to ourselves and to each other—in other words, teaching ourselves. We teach from a Diaspora in which our ways of being are mapped according to what has occurred in our external environments."[7] Alexander goes on to say of her own experience, "We were not born women of color but *became* women of color in the context of grappling with indigenous racisms within the United States and the insidious patterns of being differently positioned as black, [yellow, red,] and brown women." In other words, we become what is necessary to survive the sociopolitical circumstances of our world.

Becoming this or that sustains the sociopolitical identity and privileges or lack thereof. While many presentations of Buddhist or other spiritual teachings are concerned with releasing identity as a way to cultivate interrelationship, such an experience relies on what Alexander calls a "reciprocal investment." We all make an investment in order to enter into interrelationship or "to cross over into a metaphysics of interdependence," as Alexander says. We often avoid making such investments out of fear that it will not be reciprocated. Our distrust bears an emotional toll. How do we love when our love isn't returned?

Our interpersonal and emotional attachments to those who feel as we do are motivated by love and the need to be loved. It is often assumed that if a person looks like we do, then he or she feels as we do. Such relationships are then based on emotion. We can easily see this in teen gangs, where experiences of benign neglect lead to experiences of camaraderie centered on feelings of rage. We don't need to be teens or to be in a gang, however, to identify with each other in a similar way. Many of us create friendships and build mutual trust based on what hurts us or what might hurt us, whether we are conscious of it or not.

We also establish our sense of the self and other in relation to our emotions. We claim our anger, rage, sadness, fear, and grief. The most pervasive and fundamental emotion, from which all others surface within the lived experience of having been raced, sexualized, and gendered, is the desire to belong. The pursuit of love by way of belonging becomes our single greatest activity.

Caroline Myss, researcher in the field of human consciousness and medical intuition and author of *Anatomy of the Spirit*, says that many of us bring our stories of having been wounded with us whenever we enter a room. When we meet others, we tell them our story of suffering before we even establish any kind of relationship. The story then becomes part of our shared identity and the foundation on which the relationship exists. In other words, suffering takes center stage in emotional identities based on having been wounded. In fact, many of us who seek out spiritual sanctuaries enter them with just this type of identity, looking to be cared for. In order to elicit that care, we might continue to tell our stories of suffering. We expect that others will know about that which we have suffered, so we spend time clarifying the particulars of our circumstances. There is great disappointment when the suffering is not understood or ignored.

When leading meditation retreats I often ask students these questions:

- What is your favorite story of suffering?
- What is the story you most often tell?
- How do you tell it?
- Who is the hero?
- To whom do you tell the story and why have you chosen that person or group?
- For what reasons do you share your story?

I ask retreatants to tell their story to someone they came with or to make a friend with whom to share the same story over the eight weeks of the retreat. Each week they are to tell the story from one of the various aspects of Buddha's Eightfold Path: week one is "right view," week two is "right intention," and so on through the remaining weeks using "right speech," "right action," "right livelihood," "right effort," "right mindfulness," and "right meditation."

Storytellers are pushed to examine their stories more closely. Do we view suffering as a state that we all share each moment in interrelation, and not just as something we experience? Can we view the situation in the story from beyond our own views? Can we let go of what hooks us in the story, and suspend blame and judgment? Is our speech an expression of love or respect in the story? Are we willing to let in something new about the story that might dilute it's potency? Were our actions in the story filled with compassion and generosity, love and open-heartedness? Do we understand livelihood as being alive together and not merely as a vocation, and that the suffering has an element of mutuality? Is there a gap between ourselves and "the other" in our story? How do we use what surfaces in our world as the very source of awareness/mindfulness? How do we engage the clear mind or insights of meditation in our story?

It is an exercise in nongrasping and is meant to test the legitimacy of what we have experienced, without the exaggerations brought by the pain of it. I don't pose these questions as a psychological analysis, but to uncover and explore emotional identity on the path of liberation. These identities shape our bodies and minds. They shape the way we encounter race, sexuality, and gender. So this is an exercise in which we reveal the loving centers of our hearts in the midst of our stories of suffering. I warn retreatants that after they have told the story so many times they will either cease telling it or they will tell it out of a sense of learning, wellness, and liberation—what I call complete tenderness.

Sociopolitical and emotional identities provide us fragmented ways of looking at our lives. They are pieced together from places of possession and dispossession. It is this fragmentation, I feel, that leads some to interpret Buddhist teachings as saying that we must drop all identity for sake of wholeness. What if we instead drop the distortions that these identities bring with them and allow the bare identities to exist? Can we establish identity in relation to nature? Can identity as nature be *inclusive* of the varied forms of life in terms of race, sexuality, and gender?

··❯ **Look around you.** Look and see all the varied forms and expressions of life manifest in all living beings. The hummingbird doesn't need to detach, to let go of its form, in order to exist in a state of oneness. We don't need to drop our identities in order to exist in a state of oneness; we need only recognize the distortions and disfigurements projected onto our identities. What if we could see our unique embodiments, including our identities, as forms of nature? Can we identify with form or nature?

Granted, choosing *not* to drop identity is a departure from the view that identity is an obstacle to awakening. We are departing from requiring others to drop the labels and categories of race, sexuality, and gender, as this would end discussion of such identities. Identity is not taboo. I am not speaking of identity as a source of suffering, of illness, or as that which proves the existence of pain; rather, I am speaking of identity as a source for the experience of both personal and social awakening. I am not speaking of identity in the way it has been used to divide; rather I am speaking of a clear and undistorted identity that exists as a part of nature. I am speaking of identity that has its source in nature and not in the mind.

This type of identity resides naturally within us, just as the identity of a tree resides with it. The tree doesn't need to detach itself from being a tree to end its suffering. It is a tree in the midst of all things. If we add to the tree's identity, superimposing inferiority or superiority on it with our minds, then we would be distorting its identity and our actions would be based on a distorted appreciation of the tree. The sudden death of oak trees in where I live in Oakland is like a clear cry naturally emerging from nature, just as cries emerge from groups of people when they are ignored and mistreated. Suffering can be found as much among trees as among the people who walk beneath them.

Although the categories of race, sexuality, and gender don't grow up out of the dirt like trees, those of us who carry these identities do come from the earth and we share a system of "roots" between us. Identities are the names given to the physical forms of our inherited nature. Just as plants are identified, categorized, and named according to the physical forms they inherit, so too are human forms. This naming and labeling, however, is not the affliction of our times. What we assign to those names is what causes affliction.

When we assign superiority and inferiority to particular embodiments, we distort their identities. When we distort identity we disfigure, denigrate, and malign the natural body. When we act based on such disfigurement, we create the horrific abuse and annihilation that we see among humanity around the world. When young black males or black people in general are distortedly represented as thieves, thugs, and murderers it is easier to ignore a young black-skinned man being shot down in the street than it would be to ignore a young white-skinned woman being shot down in the same way. It is easier to take land, culture, and language from or commit genocide against a group of people when their identities, their natural appearances, have been distorted into something monstrous. We may even distort our own bodily identities, distorting our perceptions of who we are, and it is possible that this has affected the decisions we have made in our lives. Identity itself does not cause our suffering, but the distortions we bring to identity open the door to suffering.

Only when I dropped the notion that I was the creator of my own peace or oneness, or that I was powerful enough to change the world by acting to change others did I experience the way of tenderness. Peace and oneness are always there. If these elements of our true nature were not there, how could we, or any of the myriad forms of nature, be alive on this planet? We are completely supported by nature. The way of tenderness suggests that we see the body with all its variations as nature, not because it sounds lovely or seductive, but so that we will delve deeper into authentic engagement with who we are as living beings and so that we engage the reality of who we are without the need for a sense of power over each other.

All the great sages and prophets sat with their own embodied lives first, before recognizing the nature of life. No human being can see the path without first coming to an authentic awareness, in which the inevitable relationship between everything and everyone is acknowledged. There are no secrets.

••❧ The Heart Sutra, one of the key texts chanted in Zen temples throughout the world, tells us that we can leave behind the dissatisfaction of embodiment in this world by entering into the wisdom of emptiness. Trevor Leggett, in his book *The Tiger's Cave*,[8] understands the sutra to say that we should live in emptiness by emptying this human life, this world of birth and death, and living without anything in our hearts. Living in this way is to manifest the power of wisdom that dwells in the heart. "The world of birth and death" means the world of illusion and "the farther shore of wisdom" means nirvana. His reading of emptiness as "emptying the heart" resonates with the idea of body as nature.

Many mistake the teaching of emptiness to mean that we needn't speak of race, sexuality, or gender because form is emptiness. Some say we can speak of them because emptiness is form. These teachings are not about the forms that we see with our eyes. They are about the levels of our awareness of form, including our tendency to fill our hearts with notions that distort form. The message of this sutra does not emphasize emptiness as disembodied, as being without a body. When we say "living without anything in our hearts," we do not mean emptiness in the sense of zero, but rather that the heart remains clear of notions and ideas about others or about anything in life. If we can keep our hearts clear, we will be able to find compassion for others and ourselves since we will not be caught up in what has been superimposed on or internalized within our bodies. Emptiness refers to an open and uncluttered heart with regard to nature or form.

The Heart Sutra speaks to a shifting of our awareness from focusing on the concrete reality of form to an open-hearted reception of life endowed with form. If we are aware of emptiness and form, we can open-heartedly receive wisdom from the natural bodies we have inherited. The same awareness of form or of the body allows us to open-heartedly receive great compassion. The wisdom and compassion that does not distinguish between superior and inferior resides within this very body. The Heart Sutra opens us to the pure enjoyment of receiving such wisdom and compassion into our open hearts.

When we can hold "form is emptiness, emptiness is form" in this way, seeing that it points as much to form as it does to emptiness, then we will no longer relate to race, sexuality, and gender as weighty burdens but as sources for awakening as the places in which its mystery unfolds. By studying the self, seeing who you are, not only who you are in relationship to the external world or to your emotional world, but who you are as nature, you cross the waters to the other shore, to a place of tenderness.

••❧ In spiritual settings we often hear the statement "We are not our bodies." But what use is this idea to a child who is bullied at school because of having a flat nose and thick lips? What use is it to a teen who is raped for wearing clothes of the "wrong" gender? Better yet, so that there is an understanding that we are all in this dynamic relationship of life together, would we, as a society, say to a white-skinned kid who expected to gain entry to a prestigious school, but who was denied due to quotas based on race, "You are not your body"? We probably wouldn't say such a thing to an injured child, because the child shares his or her disappointments with us in search of healing, not in search of universal truths. We, too, are like injured children—hurt, agitated, and enraged because of what we have had to endure. Universal truths fall empty against such human conditions.

To simply say "We are not our bodies" is to flatten and eliminate all of the nuance that appears in teachings like the *Satipaṭṭhāna Sutta*, which teaches mindfulness of the body. The body, it says, is comprised of the five *skandhas*, or aggregates: the physical body, feelings, perceptions, mental formations, and consciousness (the five senses and thought). We are our bodies from the perspective of these conditions.

However, each of these aggregate conditions depends on the others and is interrelated to all things. So the meaning of the saying "We are not our bodies" is that we are not a singular entity but an aggregate that exists in interrelationship. "Not our bodies" means that our bodies are not ours alone, free from being conditioned by the existence of others. In fact, we are in dynamic relationship with all that lives, with all bodies. We cannot exist without the existence of all others. We are not our bodies alone. Feelings, perceptions, and consciousness do not manifest on their own. They are elements of being that appear only in relationship. Just as each aggregate does not exist in isolation, we do not exist in isolation. The aggregates are interrelated. We are interrelated.

From the point of view of our interrelationship we can say that we are not our bodies alone or that no self exists independent of others. When we operate under the delusion that we exist independent of the existence of others, we distort our sense of body and become prone to overlooking what have been deemed unacceptable differences between us. Because we do not see our bodies as all bodies, we become more prone to hatred. We turn away from our ever-present interconnectedness.

••❧ **True interrelationship means to recognize our interdependence with other living beings.** There are always others present in the field of life, whether we care to look or not. The word "true" indicates that the interrelationship we are speaking of is not just about being of the same species or about what we "do" for each other, such as grow food, build houses, provide services, or share material possessions. "Interrelationship" does not mean the cliché, "we all have a part in making the world go round." It refers to the unseen life force that is an expression of nature. It is ever present between the forms of nature, between us. What makes our interrelationship "true" is the unseen life force that exists between and sustains us. It is a collective experience of life that moves in us and between us like the breath we breathe. We cannot manipulate our interrelationship and we cannot leave it without dying. True interrelationship is like the stem from which the many pedaled layers of life flower. Without this stem at the center, the flowering of life would not occur. Can we engage awareness in race, sexuality, and gender from this center of interrelationship? Interrelationship is our core connection.

One of the greatest tragedies for humanity is that through the ages we have been replacing our unique legacy of common kinship with a superficial sense of it based on supply and demand, based on material alone. We have bypassed the expansive dynamic aspect of life by focusing on reducing and dissecting the body, and by coming to see ourselves, who or what we are, as embodied brains. We place our body parts under microscopes where they are studied and treasured—especially the brain. Meanwhile, we overlook the incredible dynamic of the unseen yet experientially available life force. We don't recognize the interrelationship at the core of life. Without recognizing or cultivating our life force as the most precious gift, we are liable to fall dormant or become extinct.

I have seen many times how the member of an elderly couple that remains behind dwindles, no matter how active they are, when they lose their spouse after decades of sharing life together. Parted from their beloved, they become frail whether they are ill or not. The power of interrelationship becomes evident the moment the other passes. It is like this, too, on the larger, collective scale. We feed off of one another. As is true throughout all of nature an unseen force of profound interrelationship sustains our existence. It is ever present.

Even if we had everything we needed, including food, water, a house, a car, clothes, and money, if there were no one else alive on the planet we would likely not live very long. We might imagine that if we had enough or more than enough we would survive. We would certainly understand when dying that the real force of life comes from the life that surrounds us. Plants in the garden know this. Thousand-year-old communities of redwood trees know this. Interrelationship is inherent to living. We experience the vivid, living power of other embodied forms—plant, animal, human—in order to survive. When we ignore this dynamic interrelationship between the various forms in nature, our life force, we devalue life. From this follows mistreatment, abuse, hatred, homicide, suicide, and genocide, and it affects everyone and everything.

••❯ **This intimate interrelationship is relevant when we consider awakening through race, sexuality, and gender by examining what we think see, hear, smell, taste, and touch.** The social dynamics of race, sexuality, and gender are formed by an interrelated consciousness built on our collective senses. Our bare physical senses engage the world without intermediary, but their consciousness is interrupted by what we have been taught about life, which we mentally impose on our experience. For example when I, as an adult woman who has learned to live in our society, see a masculine form, I see it as a man, even though this may not be true. When a relatively new baby sees the same form, it sees the form only. It does not see a male, or a man, or even a person until it has been taught to see the form as such. Because our mental sense is so deeply affected by language and what is taught, and because we rely on our educated mental capacities to navigate the world, it is difficult to perceive the unseen force of the interrelation of all life through distortions and disfigurement.

Whatever we see and hear with regard to race, sexuality, and gender has been learned. This doesn't mean that we should disengage from dialogue, however. To the contrary, it means we must engage in it more honestly so that we can unearth our ancestral and karmic tendencies and reclaim our ancient, lost kinship with one another.

⸙ **Because they interfere with how we see one another, our ancestral and karmic tendencies help to create what we learn about each other.** So we must explore the tendencies that blind us to true interrelationship. If we continue on unaware of the learned tendencies regarding race, sexuality, and gender that are stored within our collective mental lives, then our ancestral and karmic tendencies will simply ripen again to confront us with new forms of racism, heterosexism, and oppressive binary gender roles. We will continually become subject to new forms of oppression and to new notions of supremacy among living beings. Day by day the list of peoples who are pariahs will grow, and rarely will it shrink. Once placed in the category of inferior in terms of the image presented to the world by those who are "superior," rarely are any ever released.

We can choose to continue cultivating the seeds inherited from our past within these bodies or we can begin to nourish our neglected kinships. We get into the mindset in spiritual communities that any discussion of race, sexuality, and gender will unwittingly cultivate the seeds of past tendencies. Afraid of digging up those seeds, attending to them, sorting them, and replacing those that cause suffering, we may defensively say, "Let's be in the present." Might we not be cultivating the seeds of the past when we ignore them, allowing the same unruly vines to grow unattended, whether or not they are medicinal or poisonous? Can we halt the ripening of past prolonged and cruel mistreatment?

Yes we can. We can use direct, unlearned experience of kinship to sow the seeds of new ways of seeing and thinking. It is possible to cultivate an awareness of the interpretations that we bring to things and to recognize those behaviors that we learned from family, friends, and community. And we can go further than this. We can experience a spontaneous existence in which we become effortlessly aware of interrelationship, without struggling to change anything. "Not struggling to change anything" does not mean that we put an end to social movements for justice but that we give in to the spontaneous existence of relationship, rather than struggling against each other. We cease manipulating political ideology or spiritual teachings for the sake of creating a perception of oneness. In essence, it is possible to set aside the attainment of spiritual supremacy and the attainment of political power over one another, to exist personally and collectively in this ever-present, spontaneous kinship of true interrelationship.

••❧ What is the experience of spontaneous kinship between living beings? It is an experience in which we appear to and are perceived by each other, but the appearance and perception pass through our minds and hearts without stirring up the judgments of inferior and superior that we have learned to make about one another. Instead, we receive the incredible diversity of appearances and perceptions as waves and ripples in a vast ocean of interrelationship.

Our senses function on their own. We needn't cause ourselves to breathe, or make our thoughts move. Even conceptions crop up without our actively seeking them out. Likewise, identity arises spontaneously out of our bodies and minds, and spontaneously evolves in name, meaning, structure, and appearance. All of these spontaneously arising things are not fixed and isolated. They arise out of and recede back into the emptiness of our form. Our identities develop as expressions of our not truly knowing what these spontaneous appearances are, and so we name them something or someone. In recognizing the aliveness of identity, its spontaneous evolution, we see its great variance and depth. Recognizing how alive our identities are is a type of knowledge that can assist the evolution of our dialogue around race, sexuality, and gender. This knowledge helps us to release our certainty about whatever arises in the timeless moment.

Are we sure of what we see and hear? We are more likely to arouse liberated tenderness when we engage race, sexuality, and gender when we are not subsumed by identity, but rather see it with an awareness of it just as it is, without distortions or superimpositions. Even this simple act of seeing is like taking a step back—stepping back to see ourselves from a broader perspective. If I am subsumed by blackness, speaking and acting out from some idea of it, I am apt to overlook the completely mysterious unfolding of this dark flowering body. If, rather than being subsumed by blackness I could see blackness, for what it is and be aware of it, I might understand something of my life that was previously incomprehensible. By seeing the ever present quality of blackness, unproduced, without beginning or end, interrelated with everything, by letting blackness be just what it is, arising and passing away without distortion, then the tension, or even better the hypertension, associated with blackness will be lessened or eliminated.

In essence, the more we explore race, sexuality, gender, and other embodiments, the more we become conscious of how we create injustices based on super-imposed notions of superiority and inferiority. We become less likely to see the world in terms of superior or inferior, less likely to perpetuate such views, and less likely to create superficial allies or kinships. In the face of true interrelationship race, sexuality, and gender are emptied of our distortions. We can use these as places of awakening by seeing or witnessing them as they are. Learning to see our identities for what they are, we can welcome their spontaneous and dynamic evolution in our lives. When we see identity as spontaneous and evolutionary, we see that it changes depending on con-ditions and circumstances.

Identities change according to the people, times, and places that form their context. I am old enough to have gone from being colored, to Negro, to Black, to Afro-American (which was dropped when "afro" became a hairdo), to African American and/or people of Afri-can descent. The dialogue on race changed along with changes in the linguistic markers of race. Similarly, when the word "queer" came on the scene as a catch-all for "nonstraight" people, it changed the dialogue on sexuality. This form of identity newly encompassed many who did not consider themselves to be lesbian, gay, or bisexual. Nowadays, as "same-sex" marriage is being legalized in some places, this form of identity that the dialogue is taking, which upholds the binary gender construct of male and female, the term "same-sex" has left out transgender or multigendered people.

Although we can never precisely know all of the variations of identity that appear within oneness, acknowledging its spontaneous and evolutionary nature liberates us to the flowering process of interrelationship.

⋅⋅✃ There is no need to sustain interrelationship, to practice it, hold it up to see it, or to make it a superior way of thinking. We are in this interrelationship, between life and death, whether we want to recognize it or not. We can be awake to it even as we die. When I see my embodiment as nothing more than nature, nothing more than a flower, nothing to be annihilated, the experience of my life as interrelated allows tenderness to well up, despite the impositions of hatred, whether from without or within. Others may be unable to see me or those that look like me as flowers, but this does not make it any less so.

I know hate to be a product of distortions. Mostly, we are unable to see these distortions because we don't know who we really are; we have been told who we are. Fortunately, we don't need to have a near-death experience or go into any deep meditative states to access the wisdom that allows us to see clearly. If we remain still for long enough, asking ourselves what this life is, our ever-present being will step forward. We will meet each other with wordless bodies, in a deeply felt acknowledgment of tension and tenderness.

There Are No Monsters

••❧ ❧••

My father was already sixty years old when I was born. So even at a young age, I was aware of death looming over him. Riding around town in his Buick was one of our father-daughter activities. One day, I saw my father go out to the car. I waited, expecting him to call me out to take a ride with him. The minutes ticked by but he had not called me. I decided to go out and check on this ride I was expecting. I peeked into the window of the car he cherished. He was slumped over, unmoving on the seat. Was he dead?

I hesitated for a moment, before knocking on the window of the car. Slowly, Dad opened his eyes and sat up from his nap. He smiled. I smiled back. I was glad to have him back, even though I hadn't really lost him. I didn't want to have to tell Mom that he had died. Always aware of his age compared to the dads of other kids, I knew that one day someone would have to make that announcement. I secretly prayed that it wouldn't be me.

·∗⟩ ⟨∗·

"Great is the matter of birth and death, quickly pass-ing, passing, gone. Awake, awake, each one, awake! Don't waste this life." This is the message written on the *han*, a wooden instrument used in Japanese Soto Zen centers to call practitioners to the meditation hall. So when I hear the *han* sounding out, I don't hesitate; I don't waste time. I stop my mental and physical activity, listen, then walk toward the sound of the piece of wood being tapped with a wooden mallet, sounding out, "Wake up! Life is passing, right now! Right now, you are passing!"

All my life I have been working to hold on to this passing body. We are all ever vigilant with regard to protecting ourselves from death. We will all, without a doubt, lose our bodies and minds, even if we accomplish everything we want in life, even if we achieve longevity with health schemes or great refinement through religious and spiritual practices. It doesn't matter if we become enlightened or not, we will still have to experience death. Because we are born, we will also die.

Death can be both terrifying and fascinating. My own fear and curiosity at a young age became so great that I developed an intense interest in living life from a place of innermost truth. Even my ordination as a Zen priest later in life, I feel, may have come out of my childhood concerns about living and dying. It had everything to do with wanting to live this seemingly once-in-a-lifetime chance fully from the heart, from the earth.

What does death have to do with race, sexuality, and gender? It seems fitting here, at the close of this book, to return to the wisdom of poet, essayist, and philosopher Audre Lorde that I opened this book with:

> In becoming forcibly and essentially aware of my mortality, and of what I wished and wanted for my life, however short it might be, priorities and omissions became strongly etched in a merciless light, and what I most regretted were my silences. Of what had I *ever* been afraid?[9]

Lorde was dying from cancer when she wrote these words. I cried when I first read them, and I would cry every time I read them for years thereafter. I wasn't crying about my mortality. Lorde's piece is not about death as much as it is about regretting the silences: neglecting one's life and prioritizing the lives of others, devaluing one's own life experience out of fear. She's talking about self-annihilation. I knew that fear. I feared being who I was. I was afraid of hurting my family, afraid of being hated and mistreated for my entire life for loving a woman.

So when I read Lorde's testimony, over and over again, I cried about my own silence. I regretted the years of hiding, regretted not sharing that my life had been threatened in the street when it was *presumed* that I was a lesbian, regretted hiding that someone had spit in my face before. I regretted not having shared the wonderful times with the beautiful queer people in my life. Mostly, I regretted being afraid. Eventually through Zen practice and indigenous ritual, I came to respect and love my own life. When I found such respect and love my family and friends mirrored it. I am fortunate.

Like Lorde, I don't write to receive pity or an apology for the hurts imposed upon me. I write to speak up, to acknowledge the devastation wrought among us when a human life is omitted in the midst of humanity and treated as less than a treasure amid life in general.

••⊱ "I regret not having loved enough." This is a common line I've heard reported as wisdom typically delivered by a person on the verge of death. I await the moment when the deep regret about remaining silent about issues of race, sexuality, and gender rises in our hearts, and we understand what that means in terms of the systematic withholding of love from those who are different from us, then we truly come to regret not having loved enough. We will learn what it is to live with the real regret of not having attended to systemic oppression. It is this very system of silencing, ignoring, and annihilating the presence of other living beings that has wrought much of the suffering in this world. We will not have loved enough when this world comes to an end.

Death, whether our own or others, can be a powerful gateway to complete tenderness. The confrontation with the impermanence of all things is perhaps the widest gate to liberation from suffering. Facing death or dealing with death, our sight becomes clear. "Priorities and omissions are etched in a merciless light," as Lorde wrote. Given the sheer quantity of death around us, why not use this merciless light to better see who we are?

When I was thirty-nine years old it was I who received the call that my father had died in the hospital. I had long known with my childhood intuition that it would be I who would tell my mother. That Sunday I drove together with my sisters to the church where our family had worshipped with migrants from Texas and Louisiana for more than forty years. Mom was coming down the long cascading steps when I ran to meet her. She knew by the look on my face that Dad had died. Ten years later my mother would be diagnosed with a brain tumor and take the great leap into death herself. When my parents died I came to learn that despite the fact that everything appeared the same the day after as it did the day before, death, in fact, changed everything and everyone. Death widens the river's mouth, loosens our relentless grasp on life, and delivers us closer to the ultimate silence on this earth.

I came to see that the great matter of death is not great because it's scary but because it is profound in its immense capacity to arouse a loving nature within us. It brings our attention to birth as an entrance into belonging. No one should be denied this belonging, regardless of their race, sexuality, or gender. Proximity to death provides an experience by which we can see our profound lives, not as defined by vocations and careers, but as an experience of being awake.

Death seals a formidable interrelationship between all beings and all things. All things arise and cease; all beings are born and die. In death we come to know the spirit within us all. When death arrives it reminds us, like nothing else in life, that we are completely interdependent with each other. When a life is lost we lose. When, in the wake of catastrophes caused by war or weather, many are found dead in the aftermath, we see ourselves in the dead. We tremble as we connect with each other in the face of such loss.

Perhaps we can be less afraid of our differences when we realize that this merciless light of death shines upon us while we live. Perhaps we can awaken to the flow of "the river of silence" (as prophet Kahlil Gibran called death), as it courses through the vast continuum of life. This doesn't mean that we won't tremble in the presence of our fears of one another, but that we will be more present with our trembling, more awake to the truth that underlies our fears. Such was the case when I first discovered, as a child, that death is a promise that can never be broken.

We don't have to wait for death to approach to liberate ourselves from hatred. We can begin by asking ourselves, have I loved enough—within myself, within my house, beyond my doors, and into the world? Have I expressed the loving being that I am? Have I borne this love even when someone's heart is closed to it? I am not advocating love or the way of tenderness as an answer to all the ills of the world. Then again it is just that simple: to be love. We need such love to continue to confront the truth of the prolonged mistreatment that oppression brings to the world.

Race, sexuality, and gender are said to be illusions, without reality, and yet we feel their presence and hear their footsteps like invisible monsters coming at us. But there are no monsters. When we begin to treat race, sexuality, and gender—these locations of life—as much needed paths to awakening, we no longer will fear them as monsters. We are more willing to explore and engage our various embodiments when we understand them to be paths to transformation. If we do not anchor our inquiry into life within the undeniable, physical reality in which we live, spiritual awakening will remain far too abstract.

The body shapes our spiritual quest. In this book I have asked how a dark body could be transformed from a basis for oppression into a basis for spiritual awakening. What would be our quest were we given a common ground of trust and a common path of our bodies? Stillness is important. I speak of a stillness that has nothing to do with Buddha or Buddhism. I speak simply of just being still, of finding that place where our only act is breathing. In this state of stillness, we do not seek answers for our active minds but allow one breath to be the total experience of life. Dogen Zenji once said that a single moment is not a segment of life but is a whole life. A moment is *not* now; a moment is simply in a state of being itself. We, too, can be in a state of being ourselves and not worry about now. We can be wholly ourselves as ourselves while engaging the breath. As a result of this breath, as a result of the meditation that arises from it, our motivations become purified of our wounds, our expectations, our stories, and our distorted perceptions of others. Our actions begin to bubble up naturally from the well of multiplicity in oneness and interrelationship. Our actions become the spirit of social justice, in which we are all recognized as the varied expressions of nature.

··❯ When I first read the simile of the lotus growing in muddy water, I saw the mud as a problem. The simile says, just like a lotus flower that grows out of the mud and blossoms above the surface of the muddy water, we too can rise above the suffering of our lives. When I first heard this, I was not rising from the mud. I sensed myself sinking into the mud; it gathered around my ankles and began consuming me, creeping up above my waist, chest, neck, and then face, covering me until all that could be seen of me was the crown of my head. I was a sinking lotus flower.

As I returned to this simile of the lotus in the muddy water over the years I came to see it differently—I came to see the lotus as interrelated with the mud. I learned that the mud nurtures the lotus flower. The mud was not burying me; it was feeding me until I was strong enough to push through to the surface. Although systemic oppression does not feed us (quite the contrary), we need not be smothered by it. We can use it to awaken. Even while we are in the midst of it all, we can still cultivate a tender liberation. There are many people who, because there is work to do, have risen up and have not remained silent in the face of our suffering.

In her classic book *When Things Fall Apart*, Pema Chödrön says that everyone and everything is always falling apart. At times we are benefitted by personally and collectively "holding things together." Can falling apart be a liberating force in our lives? As a society we may not be ready for the way of tenderness, yet we are falling apart. We are falling into the ready-made abyss of life.

Once I was told that our good deeds at this time may not be for our own benefit and that what we are contributing today is perhaps for those who will live in the year 3000 or 4000, should humans survive that long as a species. Perhaps the way of tenderness, as a path of spiritual awakening acknowledging race, sexuality, and gender, seems futuristic. Perhaps nourishing our lost kinships seems impossible. What would we have to give up to experience such today? As Audre Lorde says, "Our silences."

Notes

1. Leah Kalmanson, "Buddhism and bell hooks: Liberatory Aesthetics and Radical Subjectivity of No-Self," in *Hypatia*, 24: 12 (2012): 810–27.
2. *The Dhammapada: The Buddha's Path of Wisdom,* translated from the Pali by Acharya Buddharakkhita, with an introduction by Bhikkhu Bodhi (Kandy: Buddhist Publication Society, 1985).
3. From the article "What's Wrong with the Term Person of Color?" by Janani. Retrieved on 3/27/2014 from http://www.blackgirldangerous.org/2013/03/2013321whats-wrong-with-the-term-person-of-color/.
4. In *Dharma, Color, and Culture: New Voices in Western Buddhism*, edited by Hilda Guttiérrez Baldoquín (Berkeley: Parallax Press, 2004).
5. When I entered the Soka Gakkai it was a part of the Nichiren Shoshu tradition. Toward the end of my stay, there was a split between the two.
6. A Zen form of practice discussion.
7. M. Jacqui Alexander, *Pedagogies of Crossing*: *Meditations on Feminism, Sexual Politics, Memory and The Sacred* (Durham: Duke University Press, 2006).
8. Trevor Leggett. *The Tiger's Cave: Translations of Japanese Zen Texts* (London: Routledge & K. Paul, 1977).
9. Audre Lorde, *Sister Outsider: Essays & Speeches* (New York: Ten Speed Press, 2007), 41.

About the Author

 **Rev. Zenju Earthlyn Manuel**, PhD, a Soto Zen priest, was born to parents who migrated from rural Louisiana and settled in Los Angeles, where she was born and raised with her two sisters. She is the author of *Sanctuary* (Wisdom Publications), and *Tell Me Something About Buddhism*, with a foreword by Thich Nhat Hanh (Hampton Roads Publishing). She is the compiler and editor of the award-winning *Seeds for a Boundless Life: Zen Teachings from the Heart* (Shambhala Publications) by Zenkei Blanche Hartman. She is contributing author to many other books including *Dharma, Color, and Culture: New Voices in Western Buddhism* (Parallax), *Hidden Lamp: Stories from Twenty-Five Centuries of Awakened Women* (Wisdom Publications), and author and illustrator of the popular *Black Angel Cards: 36 Oracle Cards and Messages for Divining Your Life* (Kasai River). For more information go to zenju.org.

Also Available
from Wisdom Publications

Dreaming Me
Black, Baptist, and Buddhist
One Woman's Spiritual Journey
Jan Willis

One of *Time* magazine's Top Religious Innovators
for the New Millennium.

The Hidden Lamp
Stories from Twenty-Five Centuries of Awakened
Women
Zenshin Florence Caplow and Reigetsu Susan Moon
Foreword by Zoketsu Norman Fischer

"An amazing collection. This book gives the wonderful feel of the sincerity, the great range, and the
nobility of the spiritual work that women are doing
and have been doing, unacknowledged, for a very
long time. An essential and delightful book."—
John Tarrant, author of *Bring Me The Rhinoceros:*
And Other Zen Koans That Will Save Your Life

Zen Women
Beyond Tea Ladies, Iron Maidens, and Macho Masters
Grace Schireson
Foreword by Miriam Levering

"An exceptional and powerful classic with great depth, humor, and clarity."—Joan Halifax, abbess of Upaya Zen Center

The Grace in Aging
Awaken as You Grow Older
Kathleen Dowling Singh

"Don't grow old without it."—Rachel Naomi Remen, MD, author of *Kitchen Table Wisdom*

Women Practicing Buddhism
American Experiences
Edited by Peter N. Gregory and Susanne Mrozik

"This accessible, clear-eyed book is a testament to how Buddhist teachings can pave the way to both social and personal liberation. Among the topics under discussion are the ordination of women, unexamined racist conditioning in predominantly white sanghas, and how women can approach patriarchal religions on their own terms."—*Tricycle*

About Wisdom Publications

Wisdom Publications is the leading publisher of classic and contemporary Buddhist books and practical works on mindfulness. To learn more about us or to explore our other books, please visit our website at wisdompubs.org or contact us at the address below.

Wisdom Publications
199 Elm Street
Somerville, Massachusetts 02144 USA

We are a 501(c)(3) organization, and donations in support of our mission are tax deductible.